D0363555

Bust of Aristotle.

the separation of governmental powers among executive, legislative, and judicial branches was the 17th-century French political theorist Montesquieu. After Montesquieu, the concept of separation of powers became one of the principal doctrines of modern constitutionalism. Nearly all modern constitutions, from the U.S. Constitution (1787) through the French Declaration of the Rights of Man and of the Citizen (1789) up to the constitutions of the post-colonial states founded in Africa and Asia in the mid-20th century provide for the separate establishment of an executive, a legislature, and a judiciary.

An important feature of constitutional government is that the functions assigned to the different branches ensure that political power is shared among them. In the U.S. system, for example, the different branches share some of the same powers insofar as each branch is able to prevent certain actions by the others—e.g., the president (the chief executive) may veto, or reject, legislation passed by Congress, the legislative branch of the federal government; the Senate (one of the two chambers of Congress, the other being the House of Representatives) may reject treaties and certain appointments made by the president; and the courts may invalidate laws passed by Congress or certain acts by the president or by executive agencies. In parliamentary forms of government such as that of the United Kingdom, power is shared through an even greater integration of the functions and even the personnel of the executive and the

In his *Politics*, the ancient Greek philosopher Aristotle distinguished among three kinds of governmental activity: the decisions of leaders or other officials, the deliberations of citizens concerning their common affairs, and the legal rulings of the courts. This threefold classification is not precisely the same as the modern distinction among the executive, legislative, and judicial functions of government. In modern states, the executive functions include formulating and directing the domestic and foreign policies of the government; the legislative functions include creating laws and (in many countries) selecting government leaders, appropriating funds, and ratifying treaties and appointments; and the judicial functions include deciding controversies over the application of the law and (in many countries) issuing authoritative interpretations of the law and determining whether existing laws or the acts of government institutions are constitutionally valid.

Another difference between Aristotle's classification and the practice of modern states is that Aristotle intended to make only a theoretical distinction among governmental functions—he stopped short of recommending that they be assigned as powers to separate institutions or branches of government. The first person to advocate

CONTENTS

Published in 2019 by Britannica Educational Publishing (a trademark of Encyclopædia Britannica, Inc.) in association with The Rosen Publishing Group, Inc.
29 East 21st Street, New York, NY 10010

Distributed exclusively by Rosen Publishing.
To see additional Britannica Educational Publishing titles, go to rosenpublishing.com.

Britannica Educational Publishing
J.E. Luebering: Executive Director, Core Editorial
Andrea R. Field: Managing Editor, Compton's by Britannica

Rosen Publishing
Carolyn DeCarlo: Editor
Nelson Sá: Art Director
Brian Garvey: Series Designer/Book Layout
Cindy Reiman: Photography Manager
Bruce Donnola: Photo Researcher

Library of Congress Cataloging-in-Publication Data

Names: Duignan, Brian, editor. | DeCarlo, Carolyn, editor.
Title: The executive branch : carrying out and enforcing laws / edited by Brian Duignan and Carolyn DeCarlo.
Description: New York : Britannica Educational Publishing, in Association with Rosen Educational Services, 2019. | Series: Checks and balances in the U.S. government | Includes bibliographical references and index. | Audience: Grades 7-12.
Identifiers: LCCN 2017053519| ISBN 9781538301647 (library book) | ISBN 9781538301654 (pbk.)
Subjects: LCSH: Presidents—United States—Juvenile literature. | Executive departments—United States--Juvenile literature. | Separation of powers—United States—Juvenile literature. | United States—Politics and government--Juvenile literature.
Classification: LCC JK517 .E84 2019 | DDC 351.73—dc23
LC record available at https://lccn.loc.gov/2017053519

Manufactured in the United States of America

CHECKS AND BALANCES
IN THE U.S. GOVERNMENT

The Executive Branch
Carrying Out and Enforcing Laws

EDITED BY BRIAN DUIGNAN AND CAROLYN DECARLO

Britannica
Educational Publishing
IN ASSOCIATION WITH
ROSEN
EDUCATIONAL SERVICES

legislature. In the nonconstitutional systems of total-
itarian or dictatorial countries, in contrast, although
there may be separate institutions such as legislatures,
executives, and judiciaries, power is not shared but
rather concentrated in a single institution. Because this
body is not subject to the checks of shared power, the
exercise of political power is uncontrolled or absolute.

The U.S. executive branch is headed by the president,
who must be a natural-born citizen of the United States,
at least 35 years old, and a resident of the country for at
least 14 years. A president is elected indirectly by the
people through an electoral college system to a four-year
term and is limited to two elected terms of office by the
Twenty-second Amendment (1951). The president's official
residence and office is the White House, located at 1600
Pennsylvania Avenue N.W. in Washington, D.C. The
formal constitutional responsibilities vested in the presidency of the United States include serving as commander
in chief of the armed forces; negotiating treaties; appointing federal judges, ambassadors, and cabinet officials; and
acting as head of state. In practice, presidential powers
have expanded to include drafting legislation, formulating
foreign policy, conducting personal diplomacy, and leading the president's political party.

The members of the president's cabinet—the attorney
general and the secretaries of State, Treasury, Defense,
Homeland Security, Interior, Agriculture, Commerce,
Labor, Health and Human Services, Housing and Urban

Development, Transportation, Education, Energy, and Veterans Affairs—are appointed by the president with the approval of the Senate; although they are described in the Twenty-fifth Amendment as "the principal officers of the executive departments," significant power has flowed to non-cabinet-level presidential aides, such as those serving in the Office of Management and Budget (OMB), the Council of Economic Advisers, the National Security Council (NSC), and the office of the White House Chief of Staff; cabinet-level rank may be conferred to the heads of such institutions at the discretion of the president. Members of the cabinet and presidential aides serve at the pleasure of the president and may be dismissed by him at any time. The executive branch also includes independent regulatory agencies such as the Federal Reserve System and the Securities and Exchange Commission.

CHAPTER ONE

THE POLITICAL EXECUTIVE

Political executives are government officials who participate in the formulation and direction of government policy. They include not only heads of state and government leaders—presidents, prime ministers, premiers, chancellors, and other chief executives—but also many secondary figures, such as cabinet members and ministers, councilors, and agency heads. In the United States and other large industrialized countries there are several thousand political executives, including the president; dozens of political appointees in the cabinet departments, in the agencies, in the commissions, and in the White House staff; and hundreds of senior civil servants.

While all positions of the executive branch, including the president, are now paid, until the Civil War, most White House servants were slaves. Moreover, the wages of all White House employees—as well as the expenses for running the White House, including staging official functions—were paid for by the president. Not until 1909 did Congress provide appropriations to pay White House servants.

THE CHIEF EXECUTIVE

The crucial element in the organization of a national executive is the role assigned to the chief executive. In presidential systems, such as in the United States, the president is both the political head of the government and also the ceremonial head of state. In parliamentary systems, such as that of the United Kingdom, the prime minister is the national political leader, but another figure, a monarch or elected president, serves as the head of state. In mixed presidential–parliamentary systems, such as that established in France under the Fifth Republic's constitution of 1958, the president serves as head of state but also wields important political powers, including the appointment of a prime minister and cabinet to serve as the government.

The manner in which the chief executive is elected or selected is often decisive in shaping his role in the political system. Thus, although he receives his seals of office from the monarch, the effective election of a British prime minister usually occurs in a private conclave of the leading members of his party in Parliament. Elected to Parliament from only one of nearly 650 constituencies, he is tied to the fortunes of the legislative majority that he leads. In contrast, the American president is elected by a nationwide electorate, and, although he leads his party's ticket, his fortunes are independent of his party. Even when the opposition party controls the Congress, his fixed term and his independent base of power allow him considerable freedom to maneuver. These contrasts explain many of the differences in the roles of the two chief executives. The British prime minister invariably has served for many years in Parliament and has developed skills in debate and in political negotiation. His major political tasks are the designation of the other members of the cabinet, the direction of parliamentary strategy, and the retention of the loyalty of a substantial majority of his legislative party. The presidential chief executive, on the other hand, often lacks prior legislative and even national-governmental experience, and his main concern is with the cultivation of a majority in the electorate through the leadership of

The current U.S. chief executive, President Donald Trump, does not have a background in politics and had not held office in the U.S. government prior to being elected president.

public opinion. Of course, since the president must have a legislative program and often cannot depend on the support of a congressional majority, he may also need the skills of a legislative strategist and negotiator.

Another important area of contrast between different national executives concerns their role in executing and administering the law. In the U.S. presidential system, the personnel of the executive branch are constitutionally separated from the personnel of Congress: no executive officeholder may seek election to either house of Congress, and no member of Congress may hold executive office. In parliamentary systems, the political management of government ministries is placed in the hands of the party leadership in parliament. In the U.S. system, the president often appoints to cabinet positions persons who have had little prior experience in politics, and may even appoint members of the opposition party. In the British system, cabinet appointments are made to consolidate the prime minister's personal ascendancy within the parliamentary party or to placate its different factions. Thus, in the U.S. system, the cabinet is responsible to the president, whereas in the British system it is responsible to the majority or governing party in Parliament. These differences extend even further into the character of the two systems of administration and the role played by civil servants. In the U.S. system, a change in administration is accompanied by the exodus of a very large number of top government executives—the political appointees who play the vital part in shaping day-to-day policy in all the departments and agencies of the national government. In Britain, when political control of the House of Commons changes, only the ministers, their parliamentary secretaries, and one or two other top political aids are replaced. For all practical purposes, the ministries remain intact and continue under the supervision of permanent civil servants.

PRESIDENTIAL SYSTEMS OF GOVERNMENT

The basic features of the U.S. presidency noted above are part of what distinguishes presidential systems of government from other systems. By definition, in a presidential system the president must originate from outside the legislative authority. In most countries, such presidents are elected directly by the citizens, though separation of origin can also be ensured through an electoral college (as in the United States), provided that legislators cannot also serve as electors. Second, the president serves simultaneously as head of government and head of state; he is empowered to select cabinet ministers, who are responsible to him and not to the legislative majority. And third, the president has some constitutionally guaranteed legislative authority: for example, the U.S. president signs into law or vetoes bills passed by Congress, though Congress may override a presidential veto with a two-thirds majority vote in both houses.

In presidential systems, the president holds power for a fixed term of office, and his authority does not depend on the strength of his party in the legislature. In many such systems, the president may be removed from office only through impeachment—in the United States this requires a vote of impeachment by a majority of the House of Representatives followed by conviction by a two-thirds majority vote of the Senate. Government officials may also be impeached in the British system; in Britain, the House of Commons acts as prosecutor and the House of Lords as judge in an impeachment proceeding. Whereas in Britain conviction on an impeachment has resulted in fines, imprisonment, and even execution, in the United States the penalties extend no further than removal and disqualification from office. In the United States the impeachment process has rarely been employed, largely because it is so cumbersome. It can occupy Congress for a lengthy period of time and involve conflicting and troublesome political pressures. Repeated attempts by Congress to amend the procedure, however, have been unsuccessful, partly because impeachment is regarded as an integral part of the system of checks and balances in the U.S. government.

Presidential systems may differ in important respects from the U.S. model. In terms of constitutional provisions, the most important variation is in the powers that the constitution delegates to the president. In contrast to the requirement that Congress needs a supermajority

The second president to be impeached was Bill Clinton (1993–2001) in 1998. He was acquitted and remained in office to serve out his term.

THE U.S. CONSTITUTION: ARTICLE II

Section 1. The executive power shall be vested in a President of the United States of America. He shall hold his office during the term of four years, and, together with the vice-president, chosen for the same term, be elected as follows:

Each state shall appoint, in such manner as the legislature thereof may direct, a number of electors, equal to the whole number of senators and representatives to which the state may be entitled in the Congress.

The electors shall meet in their respective states and vote by ballot for two persons. [...] In every case, after the choice of the President, the person having the greatest number of votes of the electors shall be the vice-president.

No person except a natural-born citizen [...] shall be eligible to the office of President; neither shall any person be eligible to that office who shall not have attained to the age of thirty-five years.

Section 2. The President shall be commander in chief of the Army and Navy of the United States. He may require the opinion, in writing, of the principal officer in each of the executive departments upon any subject relating to the duties of their respective offices. And he shall have power to grant reprieves and pardons for offenses against the United States, except in cases of impeachment.

He shall [...] nominate, and by and with the advice and consent of the Senate, shall appoint ambassadors, other public ministers and consuls, judges of the Supreme Court, and all other officers of the United States whose appointments are not herein otherwise provided for, and which shall be established by law.

Section 3. He shall from time to time give to the Congress information of the state of the Union, and recommend to their consideration such measures as he shall judge necessary and expedient.

Section 4. The President, vice-president, and all civil officers of the United States shall be removed from office on impeachment for, and conviction of, treason, bribery, or other high crimes and misdemeanors.

President Barack Obama delivers his annual State of the Union address at the U.S. Capitol in Washington, D.C., on January 20, 2015.

to override a presidential veto in the United States, for example, in some countries (e.g., Brazil and Colombia) a presidential veto may be overridden by a simple majority. Many presidential constitutions (e.g., those in Argentina, Brazil, Colombia, and Russia) explicitly give the president the authority to introduce new laws by decree, thereby bypassing the legislature, though typically the legislature can rescind such laws after the fact.

DUTIES OF THE PRESIDENT'S OFFICE

The presidency is the chief executive office of the United States. The president is vested with great authority and is arguably the most powerful elected official in the world.

The Constitution succinctly defines presidential functions, powers, and responsibilities. The president's chief duty is to make sure that the laws are faithfully executed, and this duty is performed through an elaborate system of executive agencies that includes cabinet-level departments. Presidents appoint all cabinet heads and most other high-ranking officials of the executive branch of the federal government. They also nominate all judges of the federal judiciary, including the members of the Supreme Court. Their appointments to executive and judicial posts must be approved by a majority of the Senate. The Senate usually confirms these appointments, though it occasionally rejects a nominee to whom a majority of members have strong objections.

Secretary of Treasury Steven Mnuchin speaks during a press conference in 2017. As a member of the cabinet, Mnuchin was appointed to his position by President Trump.

The president is also the commander in chief of the country's military and has unlimited authority to direct the movements of land, sea, and air forces. The president has the power to make treaties with foreign governments, though the Senate must approve such treaties by a two-thirds majority. The president has the power to sign into law or veto bills passed by Congress, though Congress can override the president's veto by summoning a two-thirds majority in favour of the measure.

CHAPTER TWO

THE HISTORICAL DEVELOPMENT OF THE U.S. PRESIDENCY

In North America, the title of president was first used for the chief magistrate of some of the British colonies. These colonial presidents were always associated with a colonial council to which they were elected, and the title of president carried over to the heads of some of the state governments (e.g., Delaware and Pennsylvania) that were organized after the start of the American Revolution in 1776. The title "President of the United States" was originally applied to the officer who presided over sessions of the Continental Congress and of the Congress established under the Articles of Confederation (1781–89). In 1787–88 the framers of the new country's Constitution created the vastly more powerful office of the presidency of the United States. The president was vested with a variety of duties and powers, including negotiating treaties with foreign governments, signing into law or vetoing legislation passed by Congress, appointing high-ranking members of the executive branch and all judges of the federal judiciary, and serving as commander in chief of the armed forces.

FOUNDATIONS IN DEMOCRACY

The nation's founders originally intended the presidency to be a narrowly restricted institution. They distrusted executive authority because their experience with colonial governors had led them to believe that executive power was inimical to liberty and that a strong executive was incompatible with the republicanism embraced in the Declaration of Independence (1776). And of course, they felt betrayed by the actions of George III, the king of Great Britain and Ireland. Accordingly, their revolutionary state constitutions provided for only nominal executive branches, and the Articles of Confederation (1781–89), the first "national" constitution, established no executive branch.

Until agreement on the electoral college, most executive powers, including the conduct of foreign relations, were held by the Senate. The delegates hastily shifted powers to the executive, and the result was ambiguous. Article II, Section 1, of the Constitution of the United States begins with a simple declarative statement: "The executive Power shall be vested in a President of the United States of America." The phrasing can be read as a blanket grant of power, an interpretation that is buttressed when the language is compared with the qualified language of Article I: "All legislative Powers herein granted shall be vested in a Congress of the United States."

This loose construction, however, is mitigated in two important ways. First, Article II itemizes, in sections two and three, certain presidential powers, including those of commander in chief of the armed forces, appointment making, treaty making, receiving ambassadors, and calling Congress into special session. Had the first article's section been intended as an open-ended authorization, such subsequent specifications would have made no sense. Second, a sizable array of powers traditionally associated with the executive, including the power to declare war, issue letters of marque and reprisal, and coin and borrow money, were given to Congress, not the president, and

The signing of the U.S. Constitution by 39 delegates to the Constitutional Convention on September 17, 1787, is depicted in this painting by Howard Chandler Christy. George Washington features prominently, standing on the right.

the power to make appointments and treaties was shared between the president and the Senate.

The delegates could leave the subject ambiguous because of their understanding that George Washington (1789–97) would be selected as the first president. They deliberately left blanks in Article II, trusting that Washington would fill in the details in a satisfactory manner. Indeed, it is safe to assert that had Washington not been available, the office might never have been created.

POSTREVOLUTIONARY PERIOD

Scarcely had Washington been inaugurated when an extraconstitutional attribute of the presidency became apparent. Inherently, the presidency is dual in character. The president serves as both head of government (the nation's chief administrator) and head of state (the symbolic embodiment of the nation). Through centuries of constitutional struggle between the crown and Parliament, England had separated the two offices, vesting the prime minister with the function of running the government and leaving the ceremonial responsibilities of leadership to the monarch. The American people idolized Washington, and he played his part artfully, striking a balance between "too free an intercourse and too much familiarity," which would reduce the dignity of the office, and "an ostentatious show" of aloofness, which would be improper in a republic.

But the problems posed by the dual nature of the office remained unsolved. A few presidents, notably Thomas Jefferson (1801–09) and Franklin D. Roosevelt (1933–45), proved able to perform both roles. More common were the examples of John F. Kennedy (1961–63) and Lyndon B. Johnson (1963–69). Although Kennedy was superb as the symbol of a vigorous nation—Americans were entranced by the image of his presidency as Camelot—he was ineffectual in getting legislation enacted. Johnson, by contrast, pushed through Congress a legislative program of major proportions, including the Civil Rights Act of 1964, but was such a failure as a king surrogate that he chose not to run for a second term.

President Lyndon B. Johnson signs the Civil Rights Act as Martin Luther King, Jr., and others look on in Washington, D.C., on July 2, 1964.

Washington's administration was most important for the precedents it set. For example, he retired after two terms, establishing a tradition maintained until 1940. During his first term, he made the presidency a full-fledged branch of government instead of a mere office. As commander in chief during the American Revolutionary War, he had been accustomed to surrounding himself with trusted aides and generals and soliciting their opinions. Gathering the department heads together seemed a logical extension of that practice, but the Constitution authorized him only to "require the Opinion, in writing" of the department heads. Taking the document literally would have precluded converting them into an advisory council. When the Supreme Court refused Washington's request for an advisory opinion on the matter of a neutrality proclamation in response to the French revolutionary and Napoleonic wars—on the ground that the court could decide only cases and not controversies—he turned at last to assembling his department heads. Cabinet meetings, as they came to be called, have remained a principal instrument for conducting executive business, though some early presidents, such as Andrew Jackson (1829–37), made little use of the cabinet.

Washington set important precedents, especially in foreign policy. In his farewell address (1796) he cautioned his successors to "steer clear of permanent alliances with any portion of the foreign world" and not to "entangle our peace and prosperity in the toils of European ambition, rivalship, interest, humor, or caprice." His warnings laid the foundation for America's isolationist foreign policy, which lasted through most of the country's history before World War II, as well as for the Monroe Doctrine.

Perils accompanying the French revolutionary wars occupied Washington's attention, as well as that of his three immediate successors. Americans were bitterly divided over the wars, some favouring Britain and its allies and others France. Political factions had already arisen over the financial policies of Washington's secretary of the treasury, Alexander Hamilton, and from 1793 onward animosities stemming from the French Revolution hardened these factions into a system of political parties, which the framers of the Constitution had not contemplated.

The emergence of the party system also created unanticipated problems with the method for electing the president. In 1796 John Adams (1797–1801), the candidate of the Federalist Party, won the presidency, and Thomas Jefferson (1801–09), the candidate of the Democratic-Republican Party, won the vice presidency; rather than working with Adams, however, Jefferson sought to undermine the administration. In 1800, to forestall the possibility of yet another divided executive, the Federalists and the Democratic-Republicans, the two leading parties of the early republic, each nominated presidential and vice presidential candidates. Because of party-line voting and the fact that electors could not indicate a presidential or vice presidential preference between the two candidates for whom they voted, the Democratic-Republican candidates, Jefferson and Aaron Burr, received an equal number of votes. The election was thrown to the House of Representatives, and a constitutional crisis nearly ensued as the House became deadlocked. Had it remained so until the end of Adams's term on March 4, 1801, Supreme Court Chief Justice John Marshall would have become president (in keeping with the existing presidential succession act). On February 17, 1801, Jefferson was finally chosen president by the House, and with the ratification of the Twelfth Amendment, beginning in 1804, electors were required to cast separate ballots for president and vice president.

THE PRESIDENCY IN THE 19TH CENTURY

Jefferson shaped the presidency almost as much as did Washington. He altered the style of the office, departing from Washington's austere dignity so far as to receive foreign ministers in run-down slippers and frayed jackets. He shunned display, protocol, and pomp; he gave no public balls or celebrations on his birthday. By completing the transition to republicanism, he humanized the presidency and made it a symbol not of the nation but of the people. He talked persuasively about the virtue of limiting government—his first inaugural address was a masterpiece on the subject—and he made gestures in that direction. He slashed the army and navy, reduced the public debt, and

Thomas Jefferson, portrait by Charles Willson Peale.

ended what he regarded as the "monarchical" practice of addressing Congress in person.

He also stretched the powers of the presidency in a variety of ways. While maintaining a posture of deference toward Congress, he managed legislation more effectively than any other president of the 19th century. He approved the Louisiana Purchase despite his private conviction that it was unconstitutional. He conducted a lengthy and successful war against the Barbary pirates of North Africa without seeking a formal declaration of war from Congress. He used the army against the interests of the American people in his efforts to enforce an embargo that was intended to compel Britain and France to respect America's rights as a neutral party during the Napoleonic wars, the ultimate goal being to bring those two countries

THE PEOPLE'S PRESIDENT

The inauguration of Andrew Jackson (1829–37), the "people's president," attracted thousands of well-wishers to the nation's capital. As Jackson rode on horseback down Pennsylvania Avenue to the White House, he was surrounded by a frenetic throng of 20,000 people, many of whom attempted to follow him into the mansion to get a better look at their hero. A contemporary, Margaret Bayer Smith, recounts what happened next:

"The halls were filled with a disorderly rabble . . . scrambling for the refreshments designed for the drawing room." While friends of the new president joined arms to protect him from the mob, "china and glass to the amount of several thousand dollars were broken in the struggle to get at the ices and cakes, though punch and other drinkables had been carried out in tubs and buckets to the people." Said Supreme Court Justice Joseph Story, "I was glad to escape from the scene as soon as possible." During his administration Jackson spent more than $50,000 refurbishing the residence, including $10,000 on decorations for the East Room and more than $4,000 on a sterling silver dinner and dessert set decorated with an American eagle.

This satirical drawing of Andrew Jackson's first reception at the White House is from *The Playfair Papers*, 1841.

to the peace table. In 1810, Jefferson compared and justified his actions to those of former President George Washington at wartime, writing: "A ship at sea in distress for provisions meets another having abundance, yet refusing a supply; the law of self-preservation authorizes the distressed to take a supply by force. In all these cases, the unwritten laws of necessity, of self-preservation, and of the public safety control the written laws of *meum* and *tuum* ['mine and thine']."

From Jefferson's departure until the end of the century, the presidency was perceived as an essentially passive institution. Only three presidents during that long span acted with great energy, and each elicited a vehement congressional reaction. Andrew Jackson exercised the veto flamboyantly; attempted, in the so-called Bank War, to undermine the Bank of the United States by removing federal deposits; and sought to mobilize the army against South Carolina when that state adopted an Ordinance of Nullification declaring the federal tariffs of 1828 and 1832 to be null and void within its boundaries. By the time his term ended, the Senate had censured him and refused to receive his messages. (When Democrats regained control of the Senate from the Whigs, Jackson's censure was expunged.)

James K. Polk (1845–49) maneuvered the United States into the Mexican War and only later sought a formal congressional declaration. When he asserted that "a state of war exists" with Mexico, Senator John C. Calhoun of South Carolina launched a tirade against him, insisting that a state of war could not exist unless Congress declared one. The third strong president during the period, Abraham Lincoln (1861–65), defending the welfare of the American people in Jeffersonian fashion, ran roughshod over the Constitution during the Civil War. But radical Republican congressmen were, at the time of his assassination, sharpening their knives in opposition to his plans for reconstructing the rebellious Southern states, and they wielded them to devastating effect against his successor, Andrew Johnson. They reduced the presidency to a cipher, demonstrating that Congress can be more powerful than the president if it acts with complete unity. Johnson was impeached on several grounds, including his violation of the Tenure of Office Act, which forbade the president from removing civil officers without the

Abraham Lincoln.

consent of the Senate. Although Johnson was not convicted, he and the presidency were badly weakened.

Contributing to the weakness of the presidency after 1824 was the use of national conventions rather than congressional caucuses to nominate presidential candidates. The new system existed primarily as a means of winning national elections and dividing the spoils of victory, and the principal function of the president became the distribution of government jobs.

CHAPTER THREE

TRANSFORMATION OF POWER

I n the 20th century, the powers and responsibilities of the presidency were transformed. President Theodore Roosevelt (1901–09) regarded the presidency as a "bully pulpit" from which to preach morality and rally his fellow citizens against "malefactors of great wealth." (And by extracting from Congress a generous fund for railroad travel, he managed to put his pulpit on wheels.) Other presidents followed Roosevelt's example, with varying results. Woodrow Wilson (1913–21) led the United States into World War I to make the world "safe for democracy," though he failed to win congressional approval for American membership in the League of Nations. Franklin D. Roosevelt was the first president to use the medium of radio effectively, and he raised the country's morale dramatically during the Great Depression. Ronald Reagan (1981–89), known as the "Great Communicator," employed televised addresses and other appearances to restore the nation's self-confidence and commit it to struggling against the Soviet Union, which he referred to as an "evil empire."

CREATING NEW PRECEDENTS

Theodore Roosevelt also introduced the practice of issuing substantive executive orders. Although the Supreme Court ruled that such orders had the force of law only if they were justified by the Constitution or authorized by Congress, in practice they covered a wide range of regulatory activity. By the early 21st century some 50,000 executive orders had been issued. Roosevelt also used executive agreements—agreements between the United States and a foreign government that are made directly by the president and are not subject to constitutional ratification by the Senate—as an alternative to treaties. The Supreme Court's ruling in *U.S.* v. *Belmont* (1937) that such agreements had the constitutional force of a treaty greatly enhanced the president's power in the conduct of foreign relations. The use of executive agreements increased significantly after 1939; whereas U.S. presidents had made 1,200 executive agreements before 1940, from that year to 1989 they made more than 13,000.

Woodrow Wilson (1913–21) introduced the notion of the president as legislator-in-chief. Although he thought of himself as a Jeffersonian advocate of limited government, he considered the British parliamentary system to be superior to the American system, and he abandoned Jefferson's precedent by addressing Congress in person, drafting and introducing legislation, and employing pressure to bring about its enactment.

Franklin D. Roosevelt (1933–45) completed the transformation of the presidency. Congress granted him unprecedented powers as part of his New Deal domestic program to raise the country out of the Great Depression; after 1937 the Supreme Court acquiesced to the changes. Through the New Deal, Roosevelt aimed at bringing about immediate economic relief as well as reforms in industry, agriculture, finance, waterpower, labor, and housing, all of which vastly increased the scope of the federal government's activities. Opposed to the traditional American political philosophy of laissez-faire, Roosevelt embraced the concept of a government-regulated economy aimed at achieving a balance between conflicting economic interests.

MILITARY SUPERPOWER

During the administration of Roosevelt's successor, Harry S. Truman (1945–53), the United States established itself as a military superpower and the U.S. presidency became the most powerful elected office in the world. In his capacity as "leader of the free world," Truman declared in 1947 that the United States would oppose communist aggression against Greece and Turkey with both economic and military aid. This policy, known as the Truman Doctrine, was followed ten years later by the Eisenhower Doctrine, declared by President Dwight D. Eisenhower (1953–61), which extended a similar guarantee of assistance to the countries of the Middle East. Yet, although he used the country's military

President Harry S. Truman awards General Dwight D. Eisenhower his fifth Distinguished Service Medal in 1952 as Mamie Eisenhower looks on. Later that year Eisenhower would be elected the 34th president of the United States.

might to defend democracy, in his farewell address, Eisenhower also warned that democracy in the United States could be undermined by the growing "military-industrial complex," which included government officials and private companies whose power or profits would be enhanced through ever-increasing military spending.

John F. Kennedy (1961–63) renewed the country's commitment to defend freedom and democracy around the world in his inaugural address (1961), declaring that "we shall pay any price, bear any burden, meet any hardship, support any friend, oppose any foe, in order to assure the survival and the success of liberty." Calling also for an end to injustice and poverty at home, he enjoined his fellow Americans: "Ask not what your country can do for you— ask what you can do for your country." Although the promise of his administration went largely unfulfilled because of his assassination in 1963, Kennedy remained an inspiring figure, especially for young people, through the 1960s and beyond. During his administration, the Twenty-third Amendment to the Constitution, which granted residents of the District of Columbia representation in the electoral college, was passed (1961).

The limits of U.S. military power and indeed the wisdom of opposing the spread of communism in all parts of the globe were severely tested during the administration of Lyndon B. Johnson (1963–69), during which the country fully committed itself to what would be a long and bloody war in Southeast Asia, the Vietnam War. Johnson arguably acquired for the executive branch the power to commit U.S. military forces to major hostilities abroad without a formal declaration of war by Congress. Truman had earlier involved U.S. troops in the Korean War without consulting Congress, but in doing so he was at least technically acting under the authority of the United Nations. The Gulf of Tonkin Resolution, passed overwhelmingly by Congress in August 1964 after dubious reports of unprovoked attacks on U.S. warships by North Vietnamese forces, declared support for the president's

THE CONSTITUTION OF THE UNITED STATES: TWENTY-THIRD AMENDMENT

Section 1. The District constituting the seat of Government of the United States shall appoint in such manner as the Congress may direct: A number of electors of President and Vice President equal to the whole number of Senators and Representatives in Congress to which the District would be entitled if it were a State, but in no event more than the least populous State; they shall be in addition to those appointed by the States, but they shall be considered, for the purposes of the election of President and Vice President, to be electors appointed by a State; and they shall meet in the District and perform such duties as provided by the twelfth article of amendment.

Section 2. The Congress shall have power to enforce this article by appropriate legislation.

determination to take all necessary measures to repel armed attacks against the forces of the United States. It was later seen as giving the president blanket authority to wage war and was repealed in 1970. Nevertheless, no subsequent U.S. military action against a foreign country has been preceded by a declaration of war, though some have occasioned congressional declarations quite similar to the Gulf of Tonkin Resolution.

Partly in reaction to the experience of the Vietnam War, Congress enacted in 1973—over a veto by President Richard Nixon—the War Powers Act, which required the executive branch to consult with and report to Congress before involving U.S. forces in foreign hostilities. The act was nonetheless resisted or ignored by subsequent presidents, most of whom regarded it as an unconstitutional usurpation of their executive authority.

THE WATERGATE SCANDAL

Presidential power remained at unprecedented levels until the mid-1970s, when Richard Nixon (1969–74) was forced to resign the office because of his role in the Watergate scandal. The Watergate affair greatly increased public cynicism about politics and elected officials, and in the 1970s and '80s it inspired legislative attempts, ultimately short-lived, to curb executive power.

The Watergate scandal concerned the revelation of illegal activities on the part of the incumbent Republican administration of President Richard M. Nixon during and after the 1972 presidential election campaign. The matter was first brought to public attention by the arrest of five men who, on June 17, 1972, broke into the headquarters of the Democratic National Committee at the Watergate office complex in Washington, D.C. Charges of burglary and wiretapping were brought against the five and against E. Howard Hunt, Jr., a former White House aide, and G. Gordon Liddy, general counsel for the Committee for the Re-election of the President. Of the seven, five pleaded guilty and two were convicted by a jury. One of the defendants, James W. McCord, Jr., charged in a letter to the court that the White House had been conducting a cover-up to conceal its connection with the break-in.

In February 1973, the Senate Select Committee on Presidential Campaign Activities, under the chairmanship of Democratic Senator Sam J. Ervin, Jr., began televised public hearings on the Watergate affair, during which former White House counsel John Dean accused

Like the rest of the nation, White House reporters tuned in to watch the televised Watergate address by President Richard Nixon on April 30, 1973.

Nixon of direct involvement in the cover-up. Other witnesses testified to acts of spying and burglary committed by a group known as the "plumbers" (because they investigated news leaks) and the use of federal agencies to harass prominent politicians, journalists, academics, and others who had been placed on Nixon's "enemies" list.

On July 16, 1973, Alexander P. Butterfield, formerly of the White House staff, disclosed that conversations in the president's offices had secretly been recorded on tape. Both Archibald Cox, the Watergate special prosecutor, and the Ervin Committee promptly subpoenaed the tapes, but Nixon refused to comply on the grounds of executive privilege and national security. Nixon eventually offered to provide written summaries of the tapes instead. After Cox rejected the proposal, Nixon ordered Attorney General Elliot L. Richardson to fire the special prosecutor. Both Richardson and William D. Ruckelshaus, deputy attorney general, resigned rather than carry out the order, and Cox was finally dismissed by a compliant solicitor general, Robert Bork.

A storm of public protest pressured Nixon into releasing seven of the nine subpoenaed tapes; one of the seven contained an 18-minute gap that, according to a later report by a panel of experts, could not have been made accidentally.

In May 1974, the House Judiciary Committee initiated a formal impeachment inquiry. On July 24, the Supreme Court ruled unanimously that Nixon must provide transcripts of additional tapes to Cox's successor as special prosecutor, Leon Jaworski. Between July 27 and 30 the House Judiciary Committee passed three articles of impeachment. On August 5 Nixon supplied transcripts of three tapes that clearly implicated him in the cover-up, and on August 8 he announced his resignation. He left office at 11:35 am the following day, August 9. He was spared punishment when his successor, Gerald R. Ford, granted him an unconditional pardon on September 8, 1974.

WAR AND POWER

Throughout the history of the United States, presidents have had vastly different approaches to international relations and the importance of peace. Whether or not they would have wished for it, war has been a looming global presence over the past six presidencies. How they've handled it—and what they've done with the powers given to them—has been a defining feature of their legacies as leaders of the nation.

REAGAN'S ANTICOMMUNISM AND THE END OF THE COLD WAR

President Ronald Reagan (1981–89) revived the notion that the United States must stop the spread of communism, particularly in the developing world, by extending military and economic assistance to threatened governments.

During his administration, military spending increased dramatically, a policy that led to huge budget deficits, but which was generally credited with hastening the collapse of the Soviet Union and the demise of eastern European communism in 1990–91.

The end of the Cold War shattered the long-standing bipartisan consensus on foreign policy and revived tensions between the executive and legislative branches over the extent of executive war-making power. The presidency also had become vulnerable again as a result of scandals and impeachment during the second term of Bill Clinton (1993–2001), and it seemed to be weakened even further by the bitter controversy surrounding the 2000 presidential election, in which Republican George W. Bush (2001–09) lost the popular vote but narrowly defeated the Democratic candidate, Vice President Al Gore, in the electoral college after the U.S. Supreme Court ordered a halt to the manual recounting of disputed ballots in Florida.

WAR ON TERROR

Events during the first year of Bush's presidency precipitated a vigorous resurgence of executive power. Following the terrorist September 11 attacks in the United States, Bush unilaterally declared an open-ended "global war on terror." In 2002 the administration announced what would become known as the Bush Doctrine: that the United States reserved the right to attack any foreign country or group it deemed a threat to its security, even without immediate provocation. A majority of Americans supported the subsequent U.S. attack on Afghanistan, whose Taliban regime had been accused of harboring al-Qaeda, the terrorist organization responsible for the September 11 attacks.

President George W. Bush discusses the September 11 terrorist attacks from aboard Air Force One, September 11, 2001.

The United States soon began transferring suspected terrorists captured in Afghanistan and elsewhere to a special prison at the U.S. naval base at Guantánamo Bay, Cuba, where some were subjected to interrogation techniques considered torturous under international law. The indefinite detention of the prisoners without charge led to several habeas corpus suits on their behalf in the federal courts. In 2002 Bush shifted his attention to Iraq, charging the government of Saddam Hussein with possessing and actively developing weapons of mass destruction (WMD) and with having ties to terrorist groups, including al-Qaeda. On Bush's order the United States led an invasion of Iraq in 2003 that quickly toppled Saddam but failed to uncover any WMD, prompting critics to charge that Bush had misled the country into war.

A SHIFT IN ATTITUDE

In an effort to improve the image of the United States abroad—damaged during the Bush administration—successor Barack Obama (2009–17) took swift steps to significantly shift this tone. Declaring his intention to put the treatment of detainees on sound legal footing, Obama signed an executive order that banned excessive and torturous interrogation techniques. He ordered the closing of the controversial military detention facility in Guantánamo Bay, Cuba, proposed a fresh start to strained relations with Russia, and traveled to Cairo to deliver a historic speech in which he reached out to the Muslim world. Largely as a result of these efforts, Obama was awarded the 2009 Nobel Peace Prize.

Despite this honour, in February 2009 Obama increased the U.S. military presence in Afghanistan to 68,000 troops. With the resurgence of the Taliban in Afghanistan, the military requested that Obama deploy an additional 40,000 troops; after carefully weighing the situation for three months, Obama chose to send an additional 30,000, a decision that was criticized by many in his party. Obama replaced the commander of NATO and U.S. forces in Afghanistan with General David Petraeus, who had been responsible for the surge strategy in Iraq. In August, the

U.S. combat mission in Iraq came to a close on schedule; though 50,000 American troops remained, the majority of U.S. forces had been withdrawn. In a televised national address marking the end of Operation Iraqi Freedom, Obama stressed the importance of American and NATO efforts in Afghanistan.

The year 2011 brought a series of world-shaking changes to the Middle East, where popular political uprisings resulted in abrupt ends to longtime authoritarian regimes in Tunisia, Egypt, and other countries in the region. While Obama resisted direct intervention in these countries, he committed U.S. forces in the form of warplanes and cruise missiles to Libya in reaction to political revolt against Muammar al-Qaddafi, which had escalated into civil war. In May, Obama made a televised address to inform the world that U.S. special forces had killed al-Qaeda leader Osama bin Laden in a firefight in Pakistan, confirmed through DNA testing.

In 2013, strained relations between Russia and the United States escalated as Russia's continued support of its ally Syria (as well as that of China) prevented the UN Security Council from responding forcefully to the Syrian Civil War. Obama, seeking to avoid open-ended involvement in another Middle Eastern conflict, had been cautious in his response to the situation in Syria. After reports surfaced of the use of chemical weapons by Syrian troops, food and financial aid from the United States were extended to the Syrian opposition in February, with the promise of military aid in June. Increasing terrorist action from the newly-formed Islamic State in Iraq and Syria (ISIS) in summer 2014 led Obama to authorize air strikes inside Syria for the first time and to increase those in Iraq.

PLOTTING A NEW COURSE

Almost immediately upon taking office in 2017, Donald Trump issued a series of executive orders designed to fulfill campaign promises. One of Trump's most controversial early executive orders, issued on January 27, implemented his promised "Muslim ban," which temporarily suspended immigration to the United States from seven Muslim-majority countries in the interest of national security. The travel ban, as it came to be known, was immediately challenged in court on due-process and establishment-of-religion grounds and provoked spontaneous demonstrations at major airports in the United States.

President Donald Trump's unique use of social media, particularly his own Twitter account, as an outlet for both personal opinion and presidential strategy complicated U.S. foreign relations, particularly regarding North Korea. Trump's presidency was also dogged by an investigation, led by former FBI director Robert Mueller, to determine whether Russia had interfered in the 2016 presidential election campaign to benefit Trump and whether members of Trump's campaign had illegally colluded with Russian officials.

CHAPTER FOUR

SELECTING A PRESIDENT

The Articles of Confederation (1781–89), the first constitution of the United States, vested the selection of the president in the legislature. Near the end of the Constitutional Convention (1787), at which a new constitution was written, the electoral college was proposed to provide a system that would select the most qualified president and vice president. Historians have suggested a variety of reasons for the adoption of the electoral college, including concerns about the separation of powers and the relationship between the executive and legislative branches, the balance between small and large states, slavery, and the perceived dangers of direct democracy.

Article II, Section 1 of the Constitution stipulated that states could select electors in any manner they desired and in a number equal to their congressional representation (senators plus representatives); the Twenty-third Amendment, adopted in 1961, provided electoral college representation for Washington, D.C. The electors would meet and vote for two people, at least one of whom could not be an inhabitant of their state. Under this plan, the person receiving the largest number of votes, provided it was a majority of the number of electors, would be elected president, and the person with the second largest number of votes would become vice president. If no one received a majority, the presidency of the United States would be decided by the House of Representatives, voting by states and choosing from among the top five candidates in the electoral vote. A tie for vice president would be broken by the Senate.

THE ELECTORAL COLLEGE

Although the framers of the Constitution established a system for electing the president, they did not devise a method for nominating presidential candidates or even choosing electors. They assumed that the selection process as a whole would be nonpartisan and devoid of factions (or political parties), which they believed were a corrupting influence in politics. The original process worked well in the early years of the republic, when George Washington, who was not affiliated closely with any faction, was the unanimous choice of electors in both 1789 and 1792. However, the rapid development of political parties soon presented a major challenge, leading to changes that would make presidential elections more partisan but ultimately more democratic as well.

Beginning in 1796, the last year of Washington's

second term, congressional caucuses, organized along party lines, met informally to select presidential and vice presidential nominees. Electors, chosen by state legislatures mostly on the basis of partisan inclination, were not expected to exercise independent judgment when voting. So strong were partisan loyalties in 1800 that all the Democratic-Republican electors voted for their party's candidates, Thomas Jefferson and Aaron Burr. Since the framers had not anticipated party-line voting and there was no mechanism for indicating a separate choice for president and vice president, the tie had to be broken by the Federalist-controlled House of Representatives. The election of Jefferson after 36 ballots led to the adoption of the Twelfth Amendment in 1804, which specified separate ballots for president and vice president and reduced the number of candidates from which the House could choose from five to three.

The development of political parties coincided with the expansion of popular choice. By 1836 all states selected their electors by direct popular vote except South Carolina, which did so only after the American Civil War. In choosing electors, most states adopted a general-ticket system in which slates of partisan electors were selected on the basis of a statewide vote. Thus, the winner of a state's popular vote would win its entire electoral vote. Only Maine and Nebraska have chosen to deviate from this method, instead allocating electoral votes to the victor in each House district and a two-electoral-vote bonus to the

Results of the U.S. presidential election of 2016.

statewide winner. The winner-take-all system generally favoured major parties over minor parties, large states over small states, and cohesive voting groups concentrated in large states over those that were more diffusely dispersed across the country.

THE EVOLUTION OF THE NOMINATION PROCESS

The word "caucus" originated in Boston in the early part of the 18th century, when it was used as the name of a political club, the Caucus, or Caucus Club. The club

THE CONSTITUTION OF THE UNITED STATES: TWELFTH AMENDMENT

The electors shall meet in their respective states and vote by ballot for President and Vice President, one of whom, at least, shall not be an inhabitant of the same state with themselves; they shall name in their ballots the person voted for as President, and in distinct ballots the person voted for as Vice President, and they shall make distinct lists of all persons voted for as President, and of all persons voted for as Vice President, and of the number of votes for each, which lists they shall sign and certify, and transmit sealed to the seat of the government of the United States, directed to the President of the Senate;—The President of the Senate shall, in the presence of the Senate and House of Representatives, open all the certificates and the votes shall then be counted;—The person having the greatest number of votes for President, shall be the President, if such number be a majority of the whole number of Electors appointed; and if no person have such majority, then from the persons having the highest numbers not exceeding three on the list of those voted for as President, the House of Representatives shall choose immediately, by ballot, the President. But in choosing the President, the votes shall be taken by states, the representation from each state having one vote; a quorum for this purpose shall consist of a member or members from two-thirds of the states, and a majority of all the states shall be necessary to a choice. The person having the greatest number of votes as Vice President, shall be the Vice President, if such number be a majority of the whole number of Electors appointed, and if no person have a majority, then from the two highest numbers on the list, the Senate shall choose the Vice President; a quorum for the purpose shall consist of two-thirds of the whole number of Senators, and a majority of the whole number shall be necessary to a choice. But no person constitutionally ineligible to the office of President shall be eligible to that of Vice President of the United States.

hosted public discussions and supported the election of candidates for public office. In its subsequent usage in the United States, the term came to denote a meeting of the managers or other officials of a political party.

Because the selection of presidential candidates after 1796 was controlled by political parties, the general public had no direct input in the process. The subsequent demise in the 1810s of the Federalist Party, which failed even to nominate a presidential candidate in 1820, made nomination by the Democratic-Republican Party caucus tantamount to election as president. This early nomination

Green Dragon Tavern, Boston, Mass., in 1773

The Green Dragon Tavern was the hub of activity for the Caucus Club in Boston, Massachusetts, depicted here in 1773.

system—dubbed "King Caucus" by its critics—evoked widespread resentment, even from some members of the Democratic-Republican caucus itself. By 1824 it had fallen into such disrepute that only one-fourth of the Democratic-Republican congressional delegation took part in the caucus that nominated Secretary of the Treasury William Crawford, instead of more popular figures such as John Quincy Adams and Andrew Jackson. Jackson, Adams, and Henry Clay eventually joined Crawford in contesting the subsequent presidential election, in which Jackson received the most popular and electoral votes but was denied the presidency by the House of Representatives (which selected Adams) after he failed to win the required majority in the electoral college. Jackson, who was particularly enraged following Adams's appointment of Clay as secretary of state, called unsuccessfully for the abolition of the electoral college, but he would get his revenge by defeating Adams in the presidential election of 1828.

In a saloon in Baltimore, Maryland, in 1832, Jackson's Democratic Party held one of the country's first national conventions (the first such convention had been held the previous year—in the same saloon—by the Anti-Masonic Party). The Democrats nominated Jackson as their presidential candidate and Martin Van Buren as his running mate and drafted a party platform. It was assumed that open and public conventions would be more democratic, but they soon came under the control of small groups of state and local party leaders, who handpicked many of the delegates. The conventions were often tense affairs, and sometimes multiple ballots were needed to overcome party divisions—particularly at conventions of the Democratic Party, which required its presidential and vice presidential nominees to secure the support of two-thirds of the delegates (a rule that was abolished in 1936).

The convention system was unaltered until the beginning of the 20th century, when general disaffection with elitism led to the growth of the Progressive movement and the introduction in some states of binding presidential primary elections to select delegates to the conventions; the primary system gave rank-and-file party members more control over the delegate-selection process. By 1916, some

20 states were using primaries, though in subsequent decades several states abolished them. From 1932 to 1968 the number of states holding presidential primaries was fairly constant (between 12 and 19), and presidential nominations remained the province of convention delegates and party bosses rather than of voters. Indeed, in 1952 Democratic convention delegates selected Adlai Stevenson as the party's nominee though Estes Kefauver had won more than three-fifths of the votes in that year's presidential primaries. In 1968, at a raucous convention in Chicago that was marred by violence on the city's streets and chaos in the convention hall, Vice President Hubert Humphrey captured the Democratic Party's presidential nomination despite his not having contested a single primary.

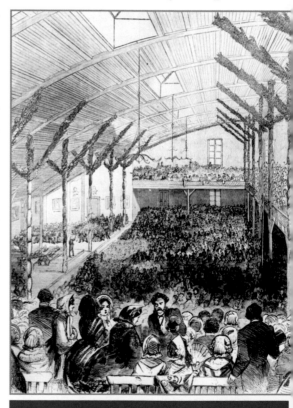

To unify the Democratic Party, Humphrey appointed a committee that proposed reforms that later fundamentally altered the

The 1860 Republican Convention in Chicago, where Abraham Lincoln was nominated for the presidency.

nomination process for both major national parties. The reforms introduced a largely primary-based system that reduced the importance of the national party conventions. Although the presidential and vice presidential candidates of both the Democratic Party and the Republican Party are still formally selected by national conventions, most of the delegates are selected through primaries—or, in a minority of states, through caucuses—and the delegates gather merely to ratify the choice of the voters.

CHAPTER FIVE

THE MODERN NOMINATION PROCESS

Although there are few constitutional requirements for the office of the presidency—presidents must be natural-born citizens, at least 35 years of age, and residents of the United States for at least 14 years—there are considerable informal barriers. No woman has yet been elected president, and all presidents but one have been Protestants (John F. Kennedy was the only Roman Catholic to occupy the office). Until Barack Obama's election as president in 2008, no ethnic minority had been a major party nominee for either the presidency or vice presidency. Successful presidential candidates generally have followed one of two paths to the White House: from prior elected office (some four-fifths of presidents have been members of the U.S. Congress or state governors) or from distinguished service in the military (e.g., Washington, Jackson, and Eisenhower).

The decision to become a candidate for president is often a difficult one, in part because candidates and their families must endure intensive scrutiny of their entire public and private lives by the news media. Before officially entering the race, prospective candidates usually organize an exploratory committee to assess their political viability. They also travel the country extensively to raise money and to generate grassroots support and favourable media exposure. Those who ultimately opt to run have been described by scholars as risk takers who have a great deal of confidence in their ability to inspire the public and handle the rigours of the office they seek.

THE MONEY GAME

Political campaigns in the United States are expensive—none more so than those for the presidency. Presidential candidates generally need to raise tens of millions of dollars to compete for their party's nomination. Even candidates facing no internal party opposition, such as incumbent presidents Bill Clinton in 1996 and George W. Bush in 2004, raise enormous sums to dissuade prospective candidates from entering the race and to campaign against their likely opponent in the general election before either party has officially nominated a candidate. Long before the first vote is cast, candidates spend much of their time fund-raising, a fact that has prompted many political analysts to claim that in reality the so-called "money primary" is the first contest in the presidential nomination process. Indeed, much of the early media coverage of a presidential campaign focuses on fund-raising, particularly at the end

THE WHITE HOUSE

The White House is the official office and residence of the president of the United States at 1600 Pennsylvania Avenue N.W. in Washington, D.C. The White House and its landscaped grounds occupy 18 acres (7.2 hectares). Since the administration of George Washington (1789–97), who occupied presidential residences in New York and Philadelphia, every American president has resided at the White House. In 1800, the entire federal government was relocated from Philadelphia to Washington. John Adams, the

The White House, Washington, D.C., as seen from the South Lawn.

country's second president (1797–1801), moved into the still unfinished presidential mansion on November 1. Following his inauguration in March 1801, Jefferson became the second president to reside in the executive mansion. In keeping with his ardent republicanism, he opened the house to public visitation each morning, a tradition that was continued (during peacetime) by all his successors. The White House is the oldest federal building in the nation's capital. The White House quickly became a focal point of the new federal city and a symbol of American democracy. The White House belonged to the people, not the president, and the president occupied it only for as long as the people allowed him to stay.

The building's history begins in 1792, when a public competition was held to choose a design for a presidential residence in the new capital city of Washington. Irish-American architect James Hoban won the commission (and a $500 prize) with his plan for a Georgian mansion in the Palladian style. The structure was to have three floors and more than 100 rooms and would be built in sandstone imported from quarries along Aquia Creek in Virginia (their colour giving the White House its name). The cornerstone was laid on October 13, 1792. Laborers, including local slaves, were housed in temporary huts built on the north side of the premises. They were joined by skilled stonemasons from Edinburgh, Scotland, in 1793.

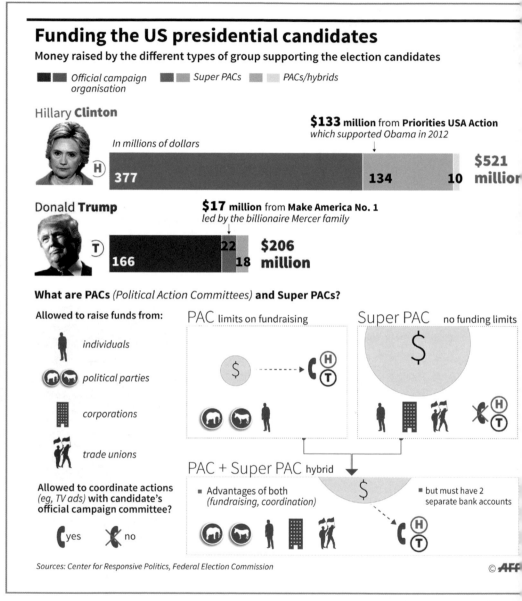

Funding the US presidential candidates

Money raised by the different types of group supporting the election candidates

- Official campaign organisation
- Super PACs
- PACs/hybrids

Hillary **Clinton**

In millions of dollars

$133 million from **Priorities USA Action**
which supported Obama in 2012

377   134   10   **$521 million**

Donald **Trump**

$17 million from **Make America No. 1**
led by the billionaire Mercer family

166   22   18   **$206 million**

What are PACs (Political Action Committees) and Super PACs?

Allowed to raise funds from:

- individuals
- political parties
- corporations
- trade unions

Allowed to coordinate actions (eg, TV ads) **with candidate's official campaign committee?**

yes   no

PAC limits on fundraising

$

Super PAC no funding limits

$

PAC + Super PAC hybrid

- Advantages of both (fundraising, coordination)
- but must have 2 separate bank accounts

$

Sources: Center for Responsive Politics, Federal Election Commission

© AFP

As this graph from the AFP global news agency illustrates, both Donald Trump and Hillary Clinton raised millions for their respective presidential campaigns in 2016.

of each quarter, when the candidates are required to file financial reports with the Federal Election Commission (FEC). Candidates who are unable to raise sufficient funds often drop out before the balloting has begun.

In the 1970s legislation regulating campaign contributions and expenditures was enacted to address increasing concerns that the largely private funding of presidential elections enabled large contributors to gain unfair influence over a president's policies and legislative agenda. Presidential candidates who agree to limit their expenditures in the primaries and caucuses to a fixed overall amount are eligible for federal matching funds, which are collected through a taxpayer "check-off" system that allows individuals to contribute a portion of their federal income tax to the Presidential Election Campaign Fund. To become eligible for such funds, candidates are required to raise a minimum of $5,000 in at least 20 states (only the first $250 of each contribution counts toward the $5,000); they then receive from the FEC a sum equivalent to the first $250 of each individual contribution (or a fraction thereof if there is a shortfall in the fund). Candidates opting to forgo federal matching funds for the primaries and caucuses, such as George W. Bush in 2000 and 2004, John Kerry in 2004, and self-financed candidate Steve Forbes in 1996, are not subject to spending limits. From 1976 through 2000, candidates could collect from individuals a maximum contribution of $1,000, a sum subsequently raised to $2,000 and indexed for inflation by the Bipartisan Campaign Reform

Act (BCRA) of 2002. (The figure was raised to $2,300 for the 2008 presidential election.)

In *Citizens United* v. *Federal Election Commission* (2010), the U.S. Supreme Court partly invalidated the BCRA by holding (5–4) that laws that prevented corporations and unions from using their general treasury funds for independent political advertising violated the First Amendment's guarantee of freedom of speech. *In SpeechNOW.org* v. *Federal Election Commission* (2010), the U.S. Court of Appeals for the District of Columbia Circuit, citing the Supreme Court's decision in *Citizens United*, struck down limits on the amounts that individuals could give to organizations that independently advocate for or against particular candidates, including by means of political advertising. One result of the SpeechNOW decision was the emergence of large ideologically driven "Super PACs" to which wealthy individuals could contribute without limit.

Despite occasional reforms, money continues to exert a considerable influence in the nomination process and in presidential elections. Although prolific fund-raising by itself is not sufficient for winning the Democratic or Republican nominations or for being elected president, it is certainly necessary.

THE PRIMARY AND CAUCUS

THE PRIMARY AND CAUCUS SEASON

Most delegates to the national conventions of the Democratic and Republican parties are selected through primaries or caucuses and are pledged to support a particular candidate. Each state party determines the date of its primary or caucus. Historically, Iowa held its caucus in mid-February, followed a week later by a primary in New Hampshire; the campaign season then ran through early June, when primaries were held in states such as New Jersey and California. Winning in either Iowa or New Hampshire—or at least doing better than expected there—often boosted a campaign, while faring poorly sometimes led candidates to withdraw. Accordingly, candidates often spent years organizing grassroots support in these states.

Primary elections may be closed (partisan), allowing only declared party members to vote, or open (nonpartisan), enabling all voters to choose which party's primary they wish to vote in without declaring any party affiliation. Primaries may also be direct or indirect. A direct primary, which is now used in some form in all U.S. states, functions as a preliminary election whereby voters decide their party's candidates. In an indirect primary, voters elect delegates who choose the party's candidates at a nominating convention.

Because of criticism that Iowa and New Hampshire were unrepresentative of the country and exerted too much influence in the nomination process, several other states began to schedule their primaries earlier. In 1988, for example, sixteen largely Southern states moved their primaries to a day in early March that became known as "Super Tuesday." Such "front-loading" of primaries and caucuses continued during the 1990s, prompting Iowa and New Hampshire to schedule their contests even earlier, in January, and causing the Democratic Party to adopt rules to protect the privileged status of the two states.

By 2008 some forty states had scheduled their primaries or caucuses for January or February; few primaries or caucuses are now held in May or June. For the 2008 campaign, several states attempted to blunt the influence of Iowa and New Hampshire by moving their primaries and caucuses to January, forcing Iowa to hold its caucus on January 3 and New Hampshire its primary on January 8. Some states, however, scheduled primaries earlier than the calendar sanctioned by the Democratic and Republican National Committees, and, as a result, both parties either reduced or, in the case of the Democrats, stripped states of their delegates to the national convention for violating party rules. For example, Michigan and Florida held their primaries on January 15 and January 29, 2008, respectively; both states were stripped of half their Republican and all their Democratic delegates to the national convention.

Front-loading has severely truncated the campaign season, requiring candidates to raise more money sooner and making it more difficult for lesser-known candidates to gain momentum by doing well in early primaries and caucuses.

PRESIDENTIAL NOMINATING CONVENTIONS

One important consequence of the front-loading of primaries is that the nominees of both major parties are now usually determined by March or April. To secure a party's nomination, a candidate must win the votes of a majority of the delegates attending the convention. (More than 4,000 delegates attend the Democratic convention, while the Republican convention usually has some 2,500 delegates.) In most Republican primaries, the candidate who wins the statewide popular vote is awarded all the state's delegates. By contrast, the Democratic Party requires that delegates be allocated proportionally to each candidate who wins at least 15 percent of the popular vote. It thus takes Democratic candidates longer than Republican candidates to amass the required majority. In 1984 the Democratic Party created a category of "superdelegates," who are unpledged to any candidate. Consisting of federal officeholders, governors, and other high-ranking party officials, they usually constitute 15 to 20 percent of the total number of delegates. Other Democratic delegates are required on the first ballot to vote for the candidate whom they are pledged to support, unless that candidate has withdrawn from consideration. If no candidate receives a first-ballot

President Dwight D. Eisenhower (*left*) and Vice President Richard Nixon accept their renomination at the 1956 Republican National Convention in San Francisco.

majority, the convention becomes open to bargaining, and all delegates are free to support any candidate. The last convention to require a second ballot was held in 1952, before the advent of the primary system.

The Democratic and Republican nominating conventions are held during the summer prior to the November general election. Shortly before the convention, the presidential candidate selects a vice presidential running mate, often to balance the ticket ideologically or geographically or to shore up one or more of the candidate's perceived weaknesses.

In the early days of television, the conventions were media spectacles, covered by the major commercial networks gavel to gavel. As the importance of the conventions declined, however, so too did the media coverage of them. Nevertheless, the conventions are still considered vital. It is at the conventions that the parties draft their platforms, which set out the policies of each party and its presidential candidate. The convention also serves to unify each party after what may have been a bitter primary season. Finally, as the nominees do not receive federal money until they have been formally chosen by the convention delegates, the conventions mark the formal start of the general election campaign, providing the candidates with a large national audience and an opportunity to explain their agendas to the American public.

The national conventions in the United States have been criticized throughout their history as undemocratic spectacles. Critics have proposed replacing them with some form of national presidential primary. By contrast, defenders argue that besides promoting party unity and enthusiasm, conventions allow compromise and tend to produce nominees and platforms that represent the political centre rather than the extremes. Because elected officials must appeal to both party leaders and the public to function effectively, supporters of conventions claim that they are a good test of how well a candidate will perform in office.

THE GENERAL ELECTION CAMPAIGN

Although the traditional starting date of the general election campaign is Labor Day (the first Monday in September), in practice the campaign begins much earlier, because the nominees are known long before the national conventions. Like primary campaigns, the general election campaign is publicly funded through the taxpayer check-off system. Since public financing was introduced in the 1970s, most Democratic and Republican candidates have opted to receive federal matching funds for the general election; in exchange for such funds, they agree to limit their spending to an amount equal to the federal matching funds they receive, plus a maximum personal contribution of $50,000. By 2004 each major party nominee received some $75 million. In 2008, Democratic nominee Barack Obama became the first presidential candidate ever to opt out of public financing for both the primary and the general election campaign; he raised more than $745 million.

Minor party presidential candidates face formidable barriers. Whereas Democratic and Republican presidential candidates are automatically listed first and second on general election ballots, minor party candidates must navigate the complex and varied state laws to gain ballot access. In addition, a new party is eligible for federal financing in an election only if it received at least 5 percent of the vote in the previous election. All parties that receive at least 25 percent of the vote in the prior presidential election are entitled to equivalent public funding.

A candidate's general election strategy is largely dictated by the electoral college system. All states except Maine and Nebraska follow the unit rule, by which all of a state's electoral votes are awarded to the candidate who receives the most popular votes in that state. Candidates therefore focus their resources and time on large states and states that are considered toss-ups, and they tend to ignore states that are considered safe for one party or the other and states with few electoral votes.

Modern presidential campaigns are media driven, as candidates spend millions of dollars on television adver-

President Carter (*left*) and his Republican challenger Ronald Reagan stand at their lecterns answering questions during their single debate in Cleveland, Ohio, 1980.

tising and on staged public events (photo ops) designed to generate favourable media coverage. The most widely viewed campaign spectacles are the debates between the Democratic and Republican presidential and vice presidential candidates. Minor parties are often excluded from such debates, a fact cited by critics who contend that the current electoral process is undemocratic and hostile to viewpoints other than those of the two major parties. First televised in 1960, such debates have been a staple of the presidential campaign since 1976. They are closely analyzed in the media and sometimes result in a shift of public opinion in favour of the candidate who is perceived to be the winner or who is seen as more attractive or personable by most viewers. Some analysts have argued, for example, that John F. Kennedy's relaxed and self-confident manner, as well as his good looks, aided him in his televised debate with Richard Nixon, contributing to his narrow victory in the presidential election of 1960. (Most who listened rather than watched, though, thought Nixon to be the winner.) Because of the potential impact and the enormous audience of the debates—some 80 million people watched the single debate between Jimmy Carter and Ronald Reagan in 1980—the campaigns usually undertake intensive negotiations over the number of debates as well as their rules and format.

The presidential election is held on the Tuesday following the first Monday in November. Voters do not actually vote for presidential and vice presidential candidates, but rather for electors pledged to a particular candidate. Only on rare occasions, such as the disputed presidential election in 2000 between Al Gore and George W. Bush, is it not clear on election day (or the following morning) who has won the presidency. Although it is possible for the candidate who has received the most popular votes to lose the electoral vote (as occurred in the 2016 election between Republican nominee Donald Trump and Democratic nominee Hillary Clinton), such inversions are infrequent. The electors gather in their respective state capitals to cast their votes on the Monday following the second Wednesday in December, and the results are formally ratified by Congress in early January.

Upon winning the election, a nonincumbent president-elect appoints a transition team to effect a smooth transfer of power between the incoming and outgoing administrations. The formal swearing-in ceremony and inauguration of the new president occurs on January 20 in Washington, D.C. The chief justice of the United States administers the formal oath of office to the president-elect: "I do solemnly swear (or affirm) that I will faithfully execute the office of President of the United States, and will to the best of my ability, preserve, protect, and defend the Constitution of the United States." The new president's first speech, called the inaugural address, is then delivered to the nation.

CHAPTER SIX

THE PRESIDENT'S CLOSEST ALLIES

Both the vice president and the first lady figure prominently in the political life of the nation. Each represents the president on official and ceremonial occasions at home and abroad. Although they have very different roles—one political and one personal—both require the president's trust, as they operate in a supportive capacity. Equally, their positioning, close to the president, places them under the scrutiny of the media and the public, who are looking for additional perspectives on the president's decision-making processes.

THE VICE PRESIDENCY OF THE UNITED STATES

The officer next in rank to the president is the vice president, who ascends to the presidency on the event of the president's death, disability, resignation, or removal. The vice president also serves as the presiding officer of the Senate, a role that is mostly ceremonial but that gives the vice president the tie-breaking vote when the Senate is deadlocked. Though famously if somewhat coarsely decried by vice president John Nance Garner as being a worthless office, fourteen vice presidents have gone on to become president. And since Garner's term as Franklin D. Roosevelt's vice president, the office has been strengthened and expanded, notably under Dick Cheney, the two-term vice president under George W. Bush.

Though Cheney never set his sights on becoming president, it is widely acknowledged that he turned the vice presidency into a more muscular and influential office. During his tenure, Cheney used his influence to help shape the administration's energy policy and foreign policy in

Vice President Dick Cheney (*left*) listens as President George W. Bush speaks to the media after meeting with the Congressional Republican leadership in the Oval Office on February 15, 2008, in Washington, D.C.

the Middle East. He played a central, controversial role in conveying the intelligence reports that Saddam Hussein of Iraq had developed weapons of mass destruction in violation of resolutions passed by the United Nations—reports used by the Bush administration to justify the Iraq War. Following the collapse of Saddam's regime, Cheney's former company, Halliburton, secured lucrative reconstruction contracts from the U.S. government, raising the specter of favouritism and possible wrongdoing—allegations that damaged Cheney's public reputation. Critics, who had long charged Cheney with being a secretive public servant, included members of Congress who brought suit against him for not disclosing records used to form the national energy policy.

Joe Biden (2009–17), vice president to Barack Obama, began his political life at the age of 29, when he was elected to the U.S. Senate (1972), becoming the fifth youngest senator in history. He went on to win reelection six times, becoming Delaware's longest-serving senator. As vice president, Biden played an active role in the administration, serving as an influential adviser to Obama and a vocal supporter of his initiatives. He helped avert several budget crises and played a key role in shaping U.S. policy in Iraq. Biden—who enjoyed high favourability ratings, partly due to a candour and affable manner that resonated with the public—did not enter the 2016 presidential election, campaigning instead for Hillary Clinton, who ultimately lost the election to Donald Trump.

Mike Pence (2017–) was named as Donald Trump's running mate in 2016 in order to help Trump with conservative voters as well as provide political experience, which the presidential candidate lacked. On November 8, 2016, the Trump-Pence ticket defeated Hillary Clinton and her running mate, Tim Kaine. Pence resigned as governor of Indiana shortly before being sworn in as vice president on January 20, 2017.

FIRST LADIES OF THE UNITED STATES

The wife of the president of the United States is known as the first lady. The president's wife has played a public role from the founding of the republic. Although the first lady's role has never been codified or officially defined, some first ladies have used their influence to affect legislation on important matters such as temperance reform, housing improvement, and women's rights.

THE FIRST FIRST LADIES

The framers of the Constitution left the chief executive considerable latitude in choosing advisers, leaving him (or her) to seek counsel from a wide variety of friends and family. When Martha Washington joined President George Washington in New York City after his inauguration, she arrived on a conspicuous barge and was greeted as a public hero. The president had already arranged to combine his office and residence in one building, thus providing her with ample opportunity to receive his callers and participate in official functions. Although she refrained from taking a stand on important issues, she was carefully watched and widely hailed as "Lady Washington."

Abigail Adams (1797–1801), the wife of John Adams, took an active part in the debate over the development of political parties, and she sometimes pointed out to her husband people she considered his enemies. While she oversaw the initial move to the new White House in Washington, D.C., in November 1800, critics focused on the political counsel she gave her husband, and some referred to her sarcastically as "Mrs President." Because Thomas Jefferson (1801–09) was a widower during his presidency, he often turned

Hand-tinted engraved portrait of American first lady and author Abigail Adams (1744–1818), late eighteenth century. She is best known for letters she wrote to her husband during the Continental Congresses and Constitutional Convention. In addition to being the wife of President John Adams, she was the mother of President John Quincy Adams.

to the wife of Secretary of State James Madison to serve as hostess. Thus, Dolley Madison had ample time (two Jefferson administrations and her husband's two terms, 1809–17) to leave a strong mark. With the assistance of architect Benjamin Latrobe, she decorated the president's residence elegantly and entertained frequently. By 1829 the outline for the job of president's wife was clear: hostess and social leader, keeper of the presidential residence, and role model for American women. When the president respected his wife's opinion (as John Adams did), she could also function as political counsel and strategist.

Among the handful of 19th-century presidential wives who sought a public role, Sarah Polk (1845–49), the wife of James Polk, was well versed in the political issues of the day and was considered a major influence on her husband. Mary Todd Lincoln (1861–65), the wife of Abraham Lincoln, though insecure in a visible role, prevailed on her husband to grant favours to friends and hangers-on. Julia Grant (1869–77), the wife of Ulysses S. Grant, was an extravagant and popular hostess during the Gilded Age and was the first of the presidents' wives to write an autobiography, though it was not published until 1975.

EXPANDING THE ROLE

Before the Civil War, the president's wife had remained a local figure, little known outside the capital, but in the last third of the 19th century she began to receive national attention. Magazines carried articles about her and the presidential family. In the 20th century—as the United States began to play a greater role in world affairs, as the president assumed increasing importance both at home and abroad, and as women's educational and job opportunities improved— the role of first lady grew considerably.

First lady for longer than any other woman, Eleanor Roosevelt (1933–45), the wife of Franklin D. Roosevelt, set new standards for how her successors would be judged. Her husband's paralysis as a result of poliomyelitis suffered in 1921 led her to travel for him, and she often said that she

Eleanor Roosevelt and Clementine Churchill, wife of the British prime minister, make a joint broadcast from the Canadian Broadcasting Corporation studios in Quebec, 1943.

acted as his "eyes and ears." She was also motivated by her early exposure to reform movements as part of a family whose involvement in liberal causes prominently featured its women as well as its men. Roosevelt was an extremely active first lady, writing articles, giving speeches, and taking stands on controversial issues. Moreover, she was widely viewed as appealing to constituencies different from her husband's, including women, African Americans, youth, the poor, and others who had formerly felt shut out of the political process. Although she regularly disclaimed any influence, she was credited with gaining appointments to important posts for many individuals from these groups. Throughout her tenure she held regular press conferences, limiting attendance to women until the start of World War II, thus ensuring that news agencies would hire more women correspondents. Her continued participation in public affairs after her husband's death further underlined the prestige she held in her own right. As a U.S. representative to the United Nations, she helped to shape the Universal Declaration of Human Rights and secure its unanimous passage. She continued to be active in the Democratic Party in the 1950s, and in 1961 President John F. Kennedy named her chair of his Commission on the Status of Women, a post she held until her death.

Jacqueline Kennedy Onassis (1961–63) was, as the wife of John F. Kennedy, the youngest first lady in 75 years. She gained enormous popularity at home and abroad because of her youth and glamour, and her two young children.

The first president's wife to name her own press secretary, she struggled to guard her privacy. Her White House renovation, aimed at restoring the mansion to its original elegance, gained wide approval. She collected and displayed items of historic and artistic value throughout its rooms. She made the White House a centre of national culture, building public interest through a televised tour of the mansion in 1962. She established the White House Historical Association, which later facilitated the mansion's official designation as a museum (1988).

President John F. Kennedy and First Lady Jacqueline Kennedy stand together in the Blue Room of the White House at Christmastime, 1961.

THE LAST HALF-CENTURY

Lady Bird Johnson (1963–69) had been a member of Washington society for nearly three decades while her husband, Lyndon B. Johnson, served in the House of

Representatives and the Senate. She took an active part in her husband's political campaigns, and during World War II had briefly run his Washington office. By the presidential election of 1960, she was such a seasoned campaigner that Robert Kennedy credited her with carrying Texas for the Democrats. In 1964, when her husband's popularity in some parts of the country was low because of his support for civil rights, she undertook a whistle-stop campaign through the South. After he won the presidential election, she spearheaded a program that resulted in the Highway Beautification Act of 1965.

Betty Ford (1974–77), the wife of Gerald R. Ford, openly expressed opinions that differed from her husband's on several important issues, including abortion. After undergoing a mastectomy for breast cancer, she insisted on telling the truth instead of concealing the matter, as some of her predecessors had done during serious illnesses. Following her example, many women went for medical examinations, a fact that, as she later wrote, made her realize the power of the first lady.

Rosalynn Carter (1977–81), the wife of Jimmy Carter, broke new ground for first ladies. Before the 1976 election, she began campaigning for her husband on her own. In 1977, soon after becoming first lady, she traveled to seven Latin American countries, where she met with political leaders and discussed substantive matters such as trade and defense. She became the first president's wife to attend cabinet meetings. She also made headlines by testifying in support of the Mental Health Systems Act before a committee of the U.S. Senate.

Hillary Rodham Clinton (1993–2001), the wife of Bill Clinton, entered the White House with a law degree, a successful career of her own, and connections to a large network of successful professionals, including other lawyers and activists. She was the first president's wife to take an office in the West Wing of the White House and was named by the president to head a task force on health care reform. Her public pronouncements on foreign policy and other issues sometimes conflicted with positions taken by her husband's administration, for which she was criticized. But her social activism, her frequent trips abroad without the president, the interviews she gave before, during,

THE HISTORY OF A HOME

During the War of 1812 the White House was burned by the British, and President James Madison (1809–17) and his family were forced to flee the city. Reconstruction and expansion began under Hoban's direction, but the building was not ready for occupancy until 1817, during the administration of President James Monroe (1817–25). Hoban's reconstruction included the addition of east and west terraces on the main building's flanks. Subsequent changes to the building in the 19th century were relatively minor. The interior was redecorated during various presidential administrations and modern conveniences were regularly added, including a refrigerator in 1845, gas lighting in 1849, and electric lighting in 1891.

During the presidency of Theodore Roosevelt, the mansion's second-floor rooms were converted from presidential offices to family living quarters. To accommodate a growing presidential staff and to provide more office space for the president, the West Wing was constructed in 1902. More office space was made available with the building of the East Wing in 1942. (The East and West wings are connected to the main building by the east and west terraces.)

At present, the White House building complex has a total of more than 130 rooms. The main building still contains the presidential family's living quarters and various reception rooms, all decorated in styles of the 18th and 19th centuries. Parts of the main building are open to the public. The west terrace contains the press briefing room, and the east terrace houses a movie theatre. The presidential office, known as the Oval Office, is located in the West Wing, as are the cabinet and press rooms; the East Wing contains other offices.

Over the years the White House has become a major American historic site, attracting more than 1.5 million visitors annually. The White House is a unit of the National Capital Parks system and was accredited as a museum in 1988.

and after her husband's impeachment, and her successful candidacy for a U.S. Senate seat from New York State in 2000 all highlighted the independent power of the first lady. In 2008, Clinton became the first first lady to attempt a bid for presidency; in December of that year, then President-elect Barack Obama selected Clinton to serve as secretary of state—another first lady

Joe Biden, vice president under President Barack Obama, swears in Hillary Rodham Clinton as secretary of state in 2009, observed by husband and former U.S. President Bill Clinton, daughter Chelsea Clinton, and mother Dorothy Rodham.

first. After serving in both terms of Obama's administration, Clinton campaigned again for presidency in the 2016 election year, this time winning the Democratic nomination. While ultimately losing to Republican nominee Donald Trump, she won the popular vote and was a memorable figure in the debates.

Laura Welch Bush (2001–09), the wife of George W. Bush, publicly disagreed with her husband's position on *Roe* v. *Wade* (1973), the U.S. Supreme Court decision that guaranteed the legality of abortion (she supported the ruling, he opposed it). She also invited writers to the White House who had openly criticized her husband, and agreed to testify before a Senate committee on education. A schoolteacher and librarian herself, she organized a national book fair to promote literacy and to encourage Americans to use libraries.

Michelle Obama (2009–17), the wife of Barack Obama, was the first African American first lady. A successful lawyer and a mother of two young children, she put her own unique stamp on the role. As first lady, she promoted volunteerism and community service, drew attention to the problems of military and working-class families, and worked to educate children on the importance of healthy eating through her public health campaign, Let's Move! which included a 2011 initiative in collaboration with Beyoncé.

Melania Trump, the wife of Donald Trump, became first lady in 2017. She was a fashion model before marrying her husband in 2005. She was only the second foreign-born first lady, the first being Louisa Adams (1825–29), the wife of John Quincy Adams.

CHAPTER SEVEN

EXECUTIVE DEPARTMENTS

I f the White House is the nerve centre of the presidency, the departments and agencies of the executive branch are the neurons. The members of the cabinet—the attorney general and the secretaries of State, Treasury, Defense, Homeland Security, Interior, Agriculture, Commerce, Labor, Health and Human Services, Housing and Urban Development, Transportation, Education, Energy, and Veterans Affairs—are appointed by the president and approved by the Senate.

THE INSTITUTION OF THE CABINET

The cabinet serves as a collective body of advisers to a chief of state, and individual members of the cabinet serve as the heads of government departments. The cabinet has become an important element of government wherever legislative powers have been vested in a parliament, but its form differs markedly in various countries, with two examples for comparison being the United Kingdom and the United States.

The cabinet system of government developed in Britain from the Privy Council in the 17th and early 18th centuries, when that body grew too large to debate affairs of state effectively. The English monarchs Charles II (reigned 1660–85) and Anne (1702–14) began regularly consulting leading members of the Privy Council in order to reach decisions before meeting with the more unwieldy full council. By the reign of Anne, the weekly, and sometimes daily, meetings of this select committee of leading ministers had become the accepted machinery of executive government, and the Privy Council's power was in inexorable decline. After George I (1714–27), who spoke little English (he was German), ceased to attend meetings with the committee in 1717, the decision-making process within that body, or cabinet, as it was now known, gradually became centred on a chief, or prime, minister. This office began to emerge during the long chief ministry (1721–42) of Sir Robert Walpole and was definitively established by Sir William Pitt later in the century.

The passage of the Reform Bill in 1832 clarified two basic principles of cabinet government: that a cabinet should be composed of members drawn from the party or political faction that holds a majority in the House of Commons and that a cabinet's members are collectively responsible to the Commons for their conduct of the government. Henceforth, no cabinet could maintain itself in power unless it had the support of a majority in the Commons. Unity in a political party proved the best way to organize support for a cabinet within the House of Commons, and the party system thus developed along with cabinet government in England.

In the United Kingdom today, the cabinet consists of about 15 to 25 members, or ministers, appointed by the prime minister, who in turn has been appointed by the monarch on the basis of his ability to command a majority of votes in the Commons. Although formerly empowered to select the cabinet, the sovereign is now restricted to the mere formal act of inviting the head of Parliament's majority party to form a government. The prime minister must put together a cabinet that represents and balances the various factions within his own party (or within a coalition of parties). Cabinet members must all be members of Parliament, as must the prime minister himself. The members of a cabinet head the principal government departments, or ministries, such as Home Affairs, Foreign Affairs, and the Exchequer (treasury). Other ministers may serve without portfolio or hold sinecure offices and are included in the cabinet on account of the value of their counsel or debating skills. The cabinet usually meets in the prime minister's official residence at 10 Downing Street in London.

Cabinet ministers are responsible for their departments, but the cabinet as a whole is accountable to Parliament for its actions, and its individual members must be willing and able to publicly defend the cabinet's policies. Cabinet members can freely disagree with each other within the secrecy of cabinet meetings, but once a decision has been reached, all are obligated to support the cabinet's policies, both in the Commons and before the general public. The loss of a vote of confidence or the defeat of a major legislative bill in the Commons can mean a cabinet's fall from power and the collective resignation of its members.

The U.S. president's cabinet is entirely different from the British-style cabinet. As noted above, it is composed of the heads of executive departments chosen by the president with the consent of the Senate, but the members do not (and cannot) hold seats in Congress, and their tenure does not depend on favourable congressional votes on administration measures. Cabinet meetings are not required under the U.S. Constitution, which in fact makes no mention of such a body. The existence of the cabinet and its operations are matters of custom rather than of law, and the cabinet as a collective body has no legal existence or power. The first American president, George Washington, began the custom of consulting regularly with his department heads as a group. The term "cabinet" was first used for the heads of the State, Treasury, and War departments by James Madison in 1793. Gradually, as administrative duties increased and different problems arose, new executive departments were created by Congress; by the early 21st century, the U.S. cabinet consisted of 15 department heads, or secretaries.

Washington's habit of calling regular and frequent cabinet meetings began a tradition that has been followed by every succeeding president. But it is important to remember that the cabinet exists solely to help the president carry out his functions as the nation's chief executive. He is virtually free to use it or not to use it as he pleases. Presidents have thus varied greatly in their use of the cabinet. Ordinarily, all members of a cabinet are of the same political party, though in recent times—as in the presidencies of Bill Clinton, George W. Bush, and Barack Obama—the administration has attempted to include at least one cabinet member of the opposition party. Attendance at U.S. cabinet meetings is not restricted exclusively to those department heads that are of cabinet rank. Cabinet appointments are for the duration of the administration, but the president may dismiss any member at his own pleasure, without approval of the Senate.

CABINET DEPARTMENTS

The U.S. cabinet is composed of the heads of 15 executive departments: Agriculture, Commerce, Defense, Education, Energy, Health and Human Services, Homeland Security, Housing and Urban Development, Interior, Justice, Labor, State, Transportation, Treasury, and Veterans Affairs.

The Department of Agriculture, also known as the USDA, is in charge of programs and policies relating to the farming industry and the use of national forests and grasslands. Formed in 1862, the USDA works to stabilize or improve domestic farm income, develop foreign markets for American agricultural products, curb poverty and hunger, protect soil and water resources, make credit available for rural development, and ensure the quality of food supplies.

The Department of Commerce is responsible for programs and policies relating to international trade, national economic growth, and technological advancement. Established in 1913, it administers the Bureau of the Census, the National Oceanic and Atmospheric Administration (NOAA), the Patent and Trademark Office, and the U.S. Travel and Tourism Administration (USTTA).

President Barack Obama meets with members of his cabinet in the Cabinet Room at the White House, 2009.

The Department of Defense is responsible for ensuring national security and supervising U.S. military forces. Based in the Pentagon building in Washington, D.C., it includes the Joint Chiefs of Staff, the departments of the U.S. Army, U.S. Navy, and U.S. Air Force, and numerous defense agencies and allied services. It was formed in 1947 by an act of Congress (amended 1949) that combined the former departments of War and the Navy.

The Department of Education is responsible for carrying out government education programs. Established in 1980 by President Jimmy Carter, it seeks to ensure access to education and to improve the quality of education nationwide. It administers programs in elementary and secondary education, higher education, vocational and adult education, special education, bilingual education, civil rights, and educational research. (The Carter family received much media attention for sending their daughter, Amy, to public school in Washington, D.C.)

The Department of Energy is responsible for administering national energy policy. Established in 1977, its most important function is to manage the country's stockpile of nuclear weapons. It also promotes energy efficiency and the use of renewable energy and develops and oversees nuclear-energy resources. Its Office of Environmental Management oversees waste management and cleanup activities at inactive facilities. The Fossil Energy Office develops policies and regulations concerning the use of natural gas, coal, and electric energy. Its regional power administrations transmit electric power produced at federal hydroelectric projects.

The Department of Health and Human Services (HHS) is responsible for carrying out government programs and policies relating to human health, welfare, and income security. Established in 1980, when responsibility for education was removed from the former Department of Health, Education, and Welfare, it consists of several agencies, including the Administration for Children and Families, the Administration on Aging, the Centers for Disease Control and Prevention, the Health Resources and Services Administration, the Indian Health Service, the National Institutes of Health, and the Substance Abuse and Mental Health Services Administration.

The Department of Homeland Security is responsible for safeguarding the United States against terrorist attacks and ensuring preparedness for natural disasters and other emergencies. In the wake of the September 11 attacks in 2001, President George W. Bush created the Office of Homeland Security to coordinate counterterrorism efforts by federal, state, and local agencies; and the Homeland Security Council to advise the president on homeland security matters. Both offices were superseded in January 2003 with the creation of the Department of Homeland Security, which assumed control of several agencies responsible for domestic security and emergency preparedness, including the Customs Service and Border Patrol (now U.S. Customs and Border Protection), the

Federal Emergency Management Agency (FEMA), the Transportation Security Administration (TSA), the Secret Service, and the Coast Guard.

The Department of Housing and Urban Development (HUD) is responsible for carrying out government housing and community-development programs. Established in 1965 under President Lyndon B. Johnson, it ensures equal access to housing and community-based employment opportunities; finances new housing, public housing, and housing rehabilitation projects; insures mortgages; and carries out programs that serve the housing needs of low-income and minority families and the elderly, the disabled, and the mentally ill. It also protects consumers against fraudulent practices by land developers, ensures the safety of manufactured homes, and defends homebuyers against abusive mortgage-loan practices.

The Department of the Interior is responsible for managing most federally owned lands and natural resources in the United States and for administering reservation communities for American Indians and Alaska Natives. Created in 1849, it encompasses the Bureau of Indian Affairs, the Bureau of Land Management, the Bureau of Reclamation, the Minerals Management Service, the Office of Surface Mining, the National Park Service, the U.S. Fish and Wildlife Service, and the U.S. Geological Survey.

The Department of Justice is responsible for the enforcement of federal laws. Headed by the U.S. attorney general, it investigates and prosecutes cases under federal antitrust, civil rights, criminal, tax, and environmental laws. It controls the Federal Bureau of Investigation (FBI), the Federal Bureau of Prisons, the Drug Enforcement Administration (DEA), the Office of Justice Programs, the U.S. Marshals Service, and the U.S. National Central Bureau of Interpol, among many other agencies.

The Department of Labor is responsible for enforcing labor statutes and promoting the general welfare of U.S. wage earners. Established in 1913, it controls the Employment Standards Administration, the Occupational Safety and Health Administration (OSHA), the Pension Benefit Guaranty Corporation, and numerous other agencies that administer programs concerned with employment and training, trade adjustment assistance, unemployment insurance, veterans and senior citizens, and mine safety.

The Department of State, also called the State Department, is responsible for carrying out U.S. foreign policy. Established in 1789, it is the oldest of the federal departments and the president's principal means of conducting treaty negotiations and forging agreements with foreign countries. Under its administration are the U.S. Mission to the United Nations, the Foreign Service Institute, and various offices of diplomatic security, foreign intelligence, policy analysis, international narcotics control, protocol, and passport services.

The Department of Transportation is responsible for programs and policies relating to transportation. Established in 1966, it controls the Federal Aviation

SECRETARY OF STATE

The head of the Department of State is known as the secretary of state. Recognized as the third most powerful position in the executive branch, the secretary of state is fourth in line to succeed the president, after the vice president, the speaker of the House of Representatives, and the president pro tempore of the Senate.

The 69th person to hold this position, Rex Tillerson, previously chairman and CEO of the Exxon Mobil Corporation (2006–16), took office on February 1, 2017, succeeding John Kerry (2013–17) in the role. Although Tillerson had no experience in the public sector, in December 2016 he was selected by President-elect Donald Trump to serve as secretary of state. Later that month he resigned from Exxon. In January 2017, his Senate confirmation hearings began; they proved highly contentious, with some senators questioning his links to Russia. However, Tillerson ultimately was confirmed, 56–43. Tillerson has also been criticized for his lack of political experience, though he was recommended by former secretary of state to President George W. Bush, Condoleezza Rice (2005–09).

Among a long list of notable secretaries beginning with Thomas Jefferson (1790–93), who went on to become the third president of the United States, John Quincy Adams (1817–25)

Secretary of State Rex Tillerson speaks to media during a press conference at Premier House on June 6, 2017, in Wellington, New Zealand, before meeting Prime Minister Bill English and Foreign Affairs Minister Gerry Brownlee.

stands out for negotiating the acquisition of Florida from Spain in 1819 and collaborating with President James Monroe on the Monroe Doctrine. William H. Seward (1861–69), who served as secretary of state to both Abraham Lincoln and Andrew Johnson, helped keep France and Britain from recognizing the Confederacy during the Civil War, successfully persuading France to withdraw troops from Mexico and negotiating the purchase of Alaska from Russia during his tenure.

The first foreign-born secretary of state, Henry Kissinger (1973–77), served both Richard Nixon and Gerald Ford. Kissinger pioneered the art of "shuttle diplomacy," travelling 560,000 miles (901,233 kilometers). The record for most countries visited in a secretary's tenure is 112 by Hillary Clinton (2009–13), followed by Madeleine Albright (1997–01), the first female secretary of state, with 96. The record for most air miles traveled in a secretary's tenure has more

(CONTINUED ON THE NEXT PAGE)

(CONTINUED FROM THE PREVIOUS PAGE)

than doubled since Kissinger's appointment, as John Kerry logged 1.38 million miles (2,220,895 km) between 2013 and 2017.

Administration (FAA), the Federal Highway Administration, the Federal Motor Carrier Safety Administration, the Federal Railroad Administration, the Federal Transit Administration, the Maritime Administration, the National Highway Traffic Safety Administration, the Pipeline and Hazardous Materials Safety Administration, and the Research and Innovative Technology Administration.

The Department of Veterans Affairs (VA) is responsible for programs and policies relating to veterans and their families. Established in 1989, it succeeded the Veterans Administration (formed in 1930). The VA administers benefits for medical care, educational assistance and vocational rehabilitation, pensions and life insurance, and payments for disability or death related to military service.

CHAPTER EIGHT

EXECUTIVE AGENCIES AND CORPORATIONS

The executive branch includes independent regulatory agencies such as the Federal Reserve System and the Securities and Exchange Commission. Governed by commissions appointed by the president and confirmed by the Senate, these agencies protect the public interest by enforcing rules and resolving disputes over federal regulations. Also part of the executive branch are government corporations (e.g., the Tennessee Valley Authority, the National Railroad Passenger Corporation [Amtrak], and the U.S. Postal Service), which supply services to consumers that could be provided by private corporations. Independent executive agencies (e.g., the Central Intelligence Agency, the National Science Foundation, and the National Aeronautics and Space Administration) comprise the remainder.

CENTRAL INTELLIGENCE AGENCY

Formally created in 1947, the Central Intelligence Agency (CIA) is the country's principal foreign intelligence and counterintelligence agency. It grew out of the World War II Office of Strategic Services (OSS). Previous U.S. intelligence and counterintelligence efforts had been conducted by the military and the Federal Bureau of Investigation (FBI) and suffered from duplication, competition, and lack of coordination.

In 1947 Congress passed the National Security Act, which created the National Security Council (NSC) and, under its direction, the CIA. Given extensive power to conduct foreign intelligence operations, the CIA was charged with advising the NSC on intelligence matters, correlating and evaluating the intelligence activities of other government agencies, and carrying out other intelligence activities as the NSC might require. Although it did not end rivalries with the military services and the FBI, the law established the CIA as the country's preeminent intelligence service.

The CIA is headed by a director and deputy director, only one of whom may be a military officer. Before the establishment of the director of National Intelligence (DNI) and the director of the Central Intelligence Agency (D/CIA) in 2005, the director of central intelligence (DCI) was responsible for managing all U.S. intelligence-gathering activities. DCIs were drawn from various fields, including not only intelligence but also the military, politics, and business. Now, the DNI serves as the chief intelligence adviser to the president and is often his close confidante.

Former Director of National Intelligence James Clapper testifies before the Senate Judiciary Committee's Subcommittee on Crime and Terrorism in the Hart Senate Office Building on Capitol Hill, May 8, 2017, in Washington, D.C.

The CIA is organized into four major directorates. The Intelligence Directorate analyzes intelligence gathered by overt means from sources such as the news media and by covert means from agents in the field, satellite photography, and the interception of telephone and other forms of communication. These analyses attempt to incorporate intelligence from all possible sources. During the Cold War in the second half of the 20th century, most of this work was focused on the military and the military-industrial complex of the Soviet Union.

The Directorate of Operations is responsible for the clandestine collection of intelligence (i.e., espionage) and special covert operations. Clandestine activities are carried out under various covers, including the diplomatic cloak used by virtually every intelligence service, as well as corporations and other "front" companies that the CIA creates or acquires. Despite the elaborate nature of some covert operations, these activities represent only a small fraction of the CIA's overall budget.

The Directorate of Science and Technology is responsible for keeping the agency abreast of scientific and technological advances, for carrying out technical operations (e.g., coordinating intelligence from reconnaissance satellites), and for supervising the monitoring of foreign media.

The Directorate of Administration is responsible for the CIA's finances and personnel matters. It also contains the Office of Security, which is responsible for the security of personnel, facilities, and information as well as for uncovering spies within the CIA.

ENVIRONMENTAL PROTECTION AGENCY

The Environmental Protection Agency (EPA) sets and enforces national pollution-control standards. In 1970, in response to ineffective environmental protection laws enacted by states and communities, President Richard Nixon created the EPA to fix, monitor, and enforce national guidelines. The EPA was initially charged with the administration of the Clean Air Act (1970), enacted to abate air pollution primarily from industries and motor vehicles; the Federal Environmental Pesticide Control Act (1972); and the Clean Water Act (1972), regulating municipal and industrial wastewater discharges and offering grants for building sewage-treatment facilities. By the mid-1990s the EPA enforced 12 major statutes, including laws designed to control uranium mill tailings; ocean dumping; toxins in drinking water; insecticides, fungicides, and rodenticides; and asbestos hazards in schools.

One of the EPA's early successes was an agreement with automobile manufacturers to install catalytic converters in cars, thereby reducing emissions of unburned hydrocarbons by 85 percent. The EPA's enforcement was in large part responsible for a decline of one-third to one-half in most air-pollution emissions in the United States from 1970 to 1990; significant improvements in water quality and waste disposal also occurred. The Comprehensive Environmental Response, Compensation, and Liability Act (also called the Superfund), providing billions of dollars for cleaning up abandoned waste dumps, was first established in 1980, but the number of those waste sites and the difficulties of the cleanups remained formidable for years thereafter.

FEDERAL RESERVE SYSTEM

The Federal Reserve System is the central banking authority of the United States. It acts as a fiscal agent for the U.S. government, is custodian of the reserve accounts of commercial banks, makes loans to commercial banks, and oversees the supply of currency, including coin, in coordination with the U.S. Mint. The system was created by the Federal Reserve Act, which President Woodrow Wilson signed into law on December 23, 1913. It consists of the Board of Governors of the Federal Reserve System, the twelve Federal Reserve banks, the Federal Open Market Committee, the Federal Advisory Council, and, since 1976, a Consumer Advisory Council; there are several thousand member banks.

The seven-member Board of Governors of the Federal Reserve System determines the reserve requirements of the member banks within statutory limits, reviews and determines the discount rates established by the twelve Federal Reserve banks, and reviews the budgets of the reserve banks. The chairman of the Board of Governors is appointed to a four-year term by the president of the United States.

Janet L. Yellen took office as chair of the Board of Governors of the Federal Reserve System on February 3, 2014, for a four-year term ending in 2018.

A Federal Reserve bank is a privately-owned corporation established pursuant to the Federal Reserve Act to serve the public interest. The 12 Federal Reserve banks are located in Boston; New York City; Philadelphia; Chicago; San Francisco; Cleveland, Ohio; Richmond, Virginia; Atlanta, Georgia; St. Louis, Missouri; Minneapolis, Minnesota; Kansas City, Missouri; and Dallas, Texas.

The 12-member Federal Open Market Committee, consisting of the seven members of the Board of Governors, the president of the Federal Reserve Bank of New York, and four members elected by the Federal Reserve banks, is responsible for the determination of Federal Reserve bank policy. The Federal Advisory Council, whose role is purely advisory, consists of one representative from each of the 12 Federal Reserve districts.

The Federal Reserve System exercises its regulatory powers in several ways, the most important of which may be classified as instruments of direct or indirect control. One form of direct control can be exercised by adjusting the legal reserve ratio—i.e., the proportion of its deposits that a member bank must hold in its reserve account—thus increasing or reducing the amount of new loans that the commercial banks can make. Because loans give rise to new deposits, the potential money supply is, in this way, expanded or reduced. The money supply may also be influenced through manipulation of the discount rate, which is the rate of interest charged by Federal Reserve banks on short-term secured loans to member banks.

Since these loans are typically sought by banks to maintain reserves at their required level, an increase in the cost of such loans has an effect similar to that of increasing the reserve requirement.

The classic method of indirect control is through open-market operations, first widely used in the 1920s and now employed daily to make small adjustments in the market. Federal Reserve bank sales or purchases of securities on the open market tend to reduce or increase the size of commercial-bank reserves; for example, when the Federal Reserve sells securities, the purchasers pay for them with checks drawn on their deposits, thereby reducing the reserves of the banks on which the checks are drawn.

NATIONAL AERONAUTICS AND SPACE ADMINISTRATION

The National Aeronautics and Space Administration (NASA) was established in 1958 to conduct research and development of vehicles and activities for the exploration of space within and outside of Earth's atmosphere.

NASA is composed of five program offices: Aeronautics and Space Technology, for the development of equipment; Space Science and Applications, dealing with programs for understanding the origin, structure, and evolution of the universe, the solar system, and the Earth; Space Flight, concerning manned and unmanned space transportation; Space Tracking and Data, involving tracking and data

Launch of the U.S. space shuttle *Discovery*, July 2006.

acquisition; and Space Station, which had a long-term goal of establishing a manned space station. A number of additional research centres are affiliated, including the Goddard Space Flight Center in Greenbelt, Maryland; the Jet Propulsion Laboratory in Pasadena, California; the Lyndon B. Johnson Space Center in Houston, Texas; and the Langley Research Center in Hampton, Virginia. The headquarters of NASA are in Washington, D.C.

NASA was created largely in response to the Soviet launching of Sputnik in 1957. NASA's organization was well under way by the early years of President John F. Kennedy's administration, when Kennedy proposed that the

United States put a man on the Moon by the end of the 1960s. To that end the Apollo program was designed, and in 1969 U.S. astronaut Neil Armstrong became the first human being to set foot on the Moon. Later unmanned programs—such as Viking, Mariner, Voyager, and Galileo—explored other bodies of the solar system.

NASA was also responsible for the development and launching of a number of satellites, including Earth-science satellites, communications satellites, and weather satellites. It also planned and developed the space shuttle, a reusable vehicle capable of carrying out missions that cannot be conducted with conventional spacecraft.

NATIONAL SECURITY COUNCIL

The National Security Council (NSC) was established by the National Security Act in 1947 to advise the president on domestic, foreign, and military policies related to national security. The president of the United States is chairman of the NSC; other members include the vice president and the secretaries of state and defense. Advisers to the NSC are the chairman of the Joint Chiefs of Staff, the director of the CIA, and other officials whom the president may appoint with Senate approval. The NSC staff is headed by a special assistant for national security affairs, who generally acts as a close adviser of the president.

OFFICE OF MANAGEMENT AND BUDGET

The Office of Management and Budget is an agency of the executive branch of the federal government that assists the president in preparing the federal budget and in supervising the budget's administration in executive agencies. It is involved in the development and resolution of all budget, policy, legislative, regulatory, procurement, and management issues on behalf of the president. The agency also evaluates the effectiveness of, and sets funding priorities for, the programs, policies, and procedures of other agencies.

SECURITIES AND EXCHANGE COMMISSION

The Securities and Exchange Commission was established by Congress in 1934 after the Senate Committee on Banking and Currency investigated the New York Stock Exchange's operations. The commission's purpose was to restore investor confidence by ending misleading sales practices and stock manipulations that led to the collapse of the stock market in 1929. It prohibited the buying of stock without adequate funds to pay for it, provided for the registration and supervision of securities markets and stockbrokers, established rules for solicitation of proxies, and prevented unfair use of nonpublic information in stock trading. It also stipulated that a company offering securities make full public disclosure of all relevant information. The commission acts as adviser to the court in corporate bankruptcy cases.

UNITED STATES POSTAL SERVICE

The United States Postal Service (USPS) is a government-owned corporation responsible for delivering mail within the United States and between the United States and other countries. Established in 1970, it replaced the Post Office Department, which had evolved from the

Former First Lady Michelle Obama and current Postmaster General Megan J. Brennan attend the Maya Angelou Forever Stamp Dedication Ceremony on April 7, 2015, in Washington, D.C.

postal system created in 1775 by the first U.S. postmaster general, Benjamin Franklin. The postal service expanded rapidly after U.S. independence. Although annual revenue also increased dramatically, the heavy cost of establishing a postal structure to keep pace with the remarkable economic progress of the country and the accelerating extension of its settled area caused expenditures to rise even faster. By the end of the 19th century, however, this expenditure had produced remarkable results. The accessibility, quality, and range of services provided had improved immeasurably.

The first supplementary postal service, registered mail, was introduced in 1855. Other milestones in this progress were postal money order service (1864); international money orders (1867); special delivery (1885); parcel post, with its accessory collect on delivery (COD) and insurances services (1913); and certified mail (1955), which provided proof of posting for items without intrinsic value. Mail was formally divided into three classes in 1863, and a fourth was added in 1879. First-class, or letter, mail is the class of mail most commonly used by the public. The other classes were established according to mail content: second-class for newspapers and magazines, third-class for other printed matter and merchandise weighing less than one pound, and fourth-class for merchandise or printed matter weighing one pound or more.

The post office has played a vital role as a pioneer and major user of all systems of transport as each was developed: the stagecoach, steamboat, canals, and railroads; the short-lived Pony Express; and airlines and motor vehicles. It also helped subsidize their development.

THE PONY EXPRESS

The Pony Express was a system of U.S. mail delivery by continuous horse-and-rider relays between St. Joseph, Missouri, and Sacramento, California, and from Sacramento to San Francisco, California, by steamer (April 1860– October 1861). Expanding Western settlement in the mid-19th century prompted the need for a reliable means of overland mail delivery. However, as national tensions simmered in advance of the Civil War (1861–65), rapid transmission of news became imperative, and the standard twenty-four-day schedule for delivery from Missouri to the West Coast was no longer sufficient.

The Pony Express route was nearly 2,000 miles (3,200 km) long overland, had about 190 stations (mostly in Nebraska, Wyoming, Utah, and Nevada), and required about 10 days to cover. Each rider generally rode 75 to 100 miles (120 to 160 km) and changed horses every 10 to 15 miles (16 to 24 km). The service (used mainly by newspapers and businesses) was remarkably efficient—during its 18 months, only one bag of mail was reported lost—but it was ultimately too expensive. It ceased with the completion of the transcontinental telegraph system.

To deal with the problem of increasing deficits and to improve the overall management and efficiency of the post office, the U.S. Congress approved the Postal Reorganization Act of 1970, signed into law August 12, 1970, which transformed the Post Office Department into a government-owned corporation, called the United States Postal Service.

CONCLUSION

Although the executive power in the federal government is vested in the president of the United States, the executive branch includes many more positions than just that of the leader of the nation. The vice president, the president's cabinet, and a number of agencies and corporations all fall under the umbrella of the executive branch, which implements and enforces the laws written by Congress. Through a series of checks and balances and separation of powers, the executive branch works alongside its two counterparts in the federal government, the legislative and judiciary branches, while maintaining that no one branch of government becomes subordinate to the other two. All three branches are interrelated, each with overlapping yet quite distinct authority, and with their roles outlined in the U.S. Constitution, the world's oldest written national constitution still in effect, and revised by the 27 amendments.

GLOSSARY

ASBESTOS Fibers that can cause asbestosis and have been implicated as causes of certain cancers, and that have been used especially formerly as fireproof insulating materials.

CAUCUS A conference of party or organization leaders (as legislators) to decide on policies, plans, appointees, and candidates.

COALITION A temporary alliance of distinct parties, persons, or states for joint action or to achieve a common purpose.

CONSTITUENCY A body of citizens or voters that is entitled to elect a representative to a legislative or other public body.

CONTENTIOUS Apt to arouse argument, conflict, or marked difference of opinion.

DELEGATE A person sent and empowered to act for another, such as a representative to a convention or conference (as of a political party).

EXPENDITURE Something that is paid out or distributed.

INCUMBENT The holder of an office or position (especially of a public nature.)

LEGISLATION The making or giving of laws (as by an individual or an organized body.)

LUCRATIVE Producing wealth; moneymaking, profitable.

MEUM AND TUUM Latin words meaning "mine"

(meum) and "thine," or "yours" (tuum).

NARCOTICS A drug (as of the opium, belladonna, or alcohol groups) that in moderate doses allays sensibility, relieves pain, and produces profound sleep but that in poisonous doses produces stupor, coma, or convulsions.

NONPARTISAN Not affiliated with or committed to the support of a particular political party; politically independent.

PRECEDENT Something done or said that may serve as an example or rule to authorize or justify a subsequent act of the same or an analogous kind; an authoritative example.

PRO TEMPORE Chosen to occupy a position either temporarily or during the absence of a regularly elected official; appointed for the time being.

PROXY The act or practice of a person serving as an authorized agent or substitute for another; the agency, function, or office of a deputy or procurator — used chiefly in the phrase "by proxy."

QUORUM The number of the members of an organized body of persons (as a legislature, court, or board of directors) that when duly assembled is legally competent to transact business in the absence of the other members; a usually specified number of members in the absence of which an organized body cannot act legally.

REGULATORY Concerned with the making of a rule or order having the force of law issued by the executive authority of a government, usually under power granted by a constitution or delegated by legislation, such as one issued by the president of the U.S. or by an authorized subordinate (also called an executive order.)

REHABILITATION The restoration of something damaged or deteriorated to a prior good condition; improvement to a higher level or greater value.

RESERVE To keep in store for future or special use.

REVENUE The annual or periodical yield of taxes, excises, customs, duties, and other sources of income that a nation, state, or municipality collects and receives into the treasury for public use.

SATELLITE A human-made object or vehicle intended to orbit the Earth, the Moon, or another celestial body and usually equipped for the transmission of space data.

SINECURE A position requiring little or no actual work, but that provides an income.

SOLICITATION The act of requesting a corporate shareholder to authorize another person or group to cast the shareholder's vote at a corporate meeting..

SUBSTANTIVE Involving matters of major or practical importance; significant.

BIBLIOGRAPHY

THE OFFICE OF THE PRESIDENT

General studies, organized historically, include Forrest McDonald, *The American Presidency: An Intellectual History* (1994); Sidney M. Milkis and Michael Nelson, *The American Presidency: Origins and Developments, 1776–2002,* 4th ed. (2003); and a classic earlier work, Edward S. Corwin, *The President: Office and Powers,* 1787–1957, 4th rev. ed. (1957).

Analyses of the office by its functions are Thomas E. Cronin, *The State of the Presidency,* 2nd ed. (1980); Louis W. Koenig, *The Chief Executive,* 6th ed. (1996); and Richard M. Pious, *The American Presidency* (1979).

A wide-ranging study by a variety of specialists is Thomas E. Cronin (ed.), *Inventing the American Presidency* (1989). An important work whose approach is indicated by its title is Arthur M. Schlesinger, Jr., *The Imperial Presidency* (1973, reissued 1998). Crucial to understanding the inner dynamics of the office is Richard E. Neustadt, *Presidential Power and the Modern Presidents,* rev. ed. (1990).

NOMINATIONS AND CAMPAIGNS

The presidential selection process and campaigns are examined in Stephen J. Wayne, *The Road to the White House, 2004: The Politics of Presidential Elections* (2004); Nelson W. Polsby and Aaron B. Wildavsky, *Presidential Elections:*

Strategies and Structures of American Politics, 11th. ed. (2004); Paul F. Boller, Jr., *Presidential Campaigns: From George Washington to George W. Bush*, 2nd rev. ed. (2004); and Kathleen Hall Jamieson, *Packaging the Presidency: A History and Criticism of Presidential Campaign Advertising*, 3rd ed. (1996). Presidential debates are comprehensively examined in Alan Schroeder, *Presidential Debates: Forty Years of High-Risk TV* (2000).

Lawrence D. Longley and Neal R. Peirce, *The Electoral College Primer 2000* (1999), is an excellent overview of the history, operation, and biases of the electoral college system. A brief but clear description of the system is Walter Berns (ed.), *After the People Vote: A Guide to the Electoral College*, rev. and enlarged ed. (1992). Critical discussion appears in Judith A. Best, *The Choice of the People?: Debating the Electoral College* (1996); and David W. Abbott and James P. Levine, *Wrong Winner: The Coming Debacle in the Electoral College* (1991).

PRESIDENTS AND FIRST LADIES

For individual presidencies, the best works are those in the American Presidency Series published by the University Press of Kansas. The leading scholarly journal in the field is *Presidential Studies Quarterly*.

Carl Sferrazza Anthony, *First Ladies*, 2 vol. (1990–91), explores the relationships among first ladies. Betty Boyd Caroli, *First Ladies*, expanded and updated ed. (2003), treats first ladies from Martha Washington to Laura Bush and discusses how their roles reflected changes in the status of women. Lewis L. Gould (ed.), *American First Ladies: Their Lives and Their Legacy*, 2nd ed. (2001), includes articles on first ladies written by experts.

THE WHITE HOUSE

Many excellent and comprehensive histories of the White House are available, including Betty Boyd Caroli, *Inside the White House: America's Most Famous Home* (1992, reissued 1999); White House Historical Association and National Geographic Society, *The White House: An Historic Guide*, 20th ed. (1999); and William Seale, *The President's House: A History*, 2 vol. (1986), and *The White House: The History of an American Idea* (1992).

THE U.S. CONSTITUTION

Cass R. Sunstein, *The Declaration of Independence and the Constitution of the United States of America* (2003), contains the full texts of the documents and a useful preface. A concise introduction is Erin Ackerman and Benjamin Ginsberg, *A Guide to the United States Constitution*, 3rd ed. (2015). John R. Vile, *A Companion to the United States Constitution and Its Amendments*, 5th ed. (2010), is a comprehensive reference work.

Catherine Drinker Bowen, *Miracle at Philadelphia* (1966, reissued 1986), examines the debates in and the events surrounding the Constitutional Convention. Books focusing on the origins of the Constitution and the intentions of its framers include Carol Berkin, *A Brilliant Solution: Inventing the American Constitution* (2002); Forrest McDonald, *Novus Ordo Seclorum: The Intellectual Origins of the Constitution* (1985); Jack N. Rakove, *Original Meanings: Politics and Ideas in the Making of the Constitution* (1996); and David Brian Robertson, *The Original Compromise: What the Constitution's Framers Were Really Thinking* (2013). Charles A. Beard, *An Economic Interpretation of the Constitution of the United States* (1913, reissued 2004), is a critical analysis of the motives of the framers.

INDEX